OSBORNE & LITTLE

style

OSBORNE & LITTLE
style

JACKIE COLE

A BULFINCH PRESS BOOK
LITTLE, BROWN AND COMPANY

BOSTON   NEW YORK   TORONTO   LONDON

Foreword

BY PETER OSBORNE AND ANTONY LITTLE

This is a book of ideas, of inspirations. It won't tell you how to make pinch pleat headings or quilted cushion covers. Nor does it attempt to relate the history of interior decorating, a subject copiously covered elsewhere.

But it will show you examples, many examples, of how to use our fabrics, papers and trimmings in unusual, distinctive ways. Rooms by many leading decorators are featured, and, of course, our own homes. We hope that you will try out for yourself some of the ideas in the pages that follow; even perhaps take them further, for, in the end, a scheme that reflects your own taste and individuality is far more rewarding.

We believe that imagination is a key element in interior design. That inspired combination of old and new, of pattern, colour and texture, often breaking rules, is what lifts the decoration of a room above the merely mundane to become unique and stunning. Eccentric and eclectic in the best British tradition – that is the Osborne & Little style. Style is an unobtrusive quality; perhaps you only recognize it when it's absent. In the book's three main chapters – Classic, City and Country – it's here, in abundance.

Our thanks to Felicity Osborne who has played a key role in bringing this book to life and who masterminds our advertising (see left) and to Jackie Cole who wrote everything but this foreword.

INTRODUCTION

The Beginnings

When Osborne & Little's first collection of hand-printed wallpapers burst onto the decorating scene in 1968, the bold designs captured the imagination of a public immersed in the 'swinging sixties' and hungry for innovation.

The founding duo, Peter Osborne and Antony Little, were brothers-in-law with quite different backgrounds. Peter, after Oxford University and an unstimulating year in merchant banking, was determined to start his own business. Antony, a Fine Arts graduate from Kingston College of Art, was gaining a growing reputation as a book illustrator and interior decorator, involved in exciting projects such as the flagship Biba store in London. They pooled their talents and resources and set up business in a converted locksmith's shop in London's Brompton Cross, flanked by trend-setting boutiques.

EARLY DAYS

The first Osborne & Little collection drew on sources as diverse as Moorish architecture, the Brighton Pavilion and the swirling foliage of Art Nouveau for its inspirations. These extravagant designs, which were outlined in gold and silver and printed on thick coloured papers in vibrant reds, blues, greens and earthy browns, were an immediate success and won the most prestigious design prize of the time, The Council of Industrial Design Award.

Since those heady and frenetic days, the home furnishings industry has changed beyond all recognition. Interior decoration, once the domain of the fashionable few, now has universal appeal as awareness of good design has flourished. Osborne & Little has grown up, too, in the intervening years.

The early 1970s saw them move to the present showroom on London's King's Road, and expand their collections beyond wallpapers into printed and woven fabrics. Indeed, these now represent some three-quarters of total sales. Early in the 1980s, the print works, design studio and offices moved to larger premises in south London, where they are still based today.

The year 1985 was an important one for Osborne & Little. They became a publicly quoted company with their shares listed on the Stock Exchange, albeit with the founding partners retaining control. They also set up their American subsidiary, which now accounts for some forty per cent of overall business.

In addition to the Osborne & Little studio collections, the company has, since 1989, distributed the collections of Nina Campbell, one of the country's foremost decorators, and, since 1996, the collections of Liberty Furnishings. This mix of styling and colouring makes for a rich and comprehensive choice.

From a small family-run enterprise, Osborne & Little has developed into an international company, but the approach remains emphatically hands-on, with Antony still designing and Peter still managing.

INNOVATIVE SPIRIT

Osborne & Little may have become part of the establishment but it continues to be very much at the leading edge of the industry, and the innovative spirit that characterized the early years continues unabated today. Many established trends, such as paint effects on wallpaper, and star and topiary patterns, first saw daylight in the Osborne & Little studio. This studio of skilled designers and colourists, under the creative guidance of Antony Little, produces a dozen or so

provided the inspiration and starting points for individual designs, and in some cases, even whole collections.

A CONTEMPORARY EDGE

While the inspiration may be classical or documentary in derivation, the interpretation usually has a contemporary edge to it. Traditional tartans are woven in silks, damasks are reworked in unusual colours, velvet corduroys upholster modern furniture, fresh renditions and recolourings radically change appearances. It is this commitment to both classic and contemporary styles that has established Osborne & Little as leaders in British interior design.

CHAPTER ONE

Classic ◆◆◆

THE CLASSIC INTERIOR owes as much to an awareness of the present as it does to a retrospective look at the past. This unique mixture of an appreciation of new trends and techniques combined with an air of nostalgia is the essence of successful traditional decorating. Over the past sixty years, English decorators have been inspired by the styles of the eighteenth and early-nineteenth centuries, and their often highly individual interpretations of this rich tradition epitomize classic style today. No two classic rooms will ever be the same, for every decorator will always place his or her own individual stamp on a scheme. Yet the finished look is invariably timeless; the influence of the great decorators of this century and the great houses of the past is never far away.

American designers share the English decorators love of richly textured fabrics, damasks, silks and weaves, but often use them in a subtly different way. In the United States, the most successful interpretations of classic style are those which subtly combine elements of English taste with more indigenous characteristics. The houses of Long Island, for example, where chintz is mixed with plantation shutters and cool stripes and checks, have a distinctive style that has made its mark on both sides of the Atlantic.

ABOVE LEFT: *Red chenille is battened onto the walls of Christopher Vane Percy's drawing room.*

ABOVE: *Chenille tassels contrast effectively with the plain and striped seersucker silk curtains.*

OPPOSITE: *On a swagged dress curtain, red shot silk contrasts with a striped seersucker silk lining.*

PRECEDING PAGES (MAIN PICTURE AND INSET): *A restored Regency chaise covered in slub dupion silk epitomizes urban elegance.*

OPPOSITE: *The drawing room of Antony Little's London flat is dominated by classically swagged and tailed green silk damask curtains, caught with rosettes and embellished with a natural-coloured cotton fringe.*

RIGHT AND BELOW: *The drawing room has a strong architectural quality with its dentil cornice and Palladian details. The strict symmetry of furniture, lamps and pictures echoes this classical formality. A pair of matching camel-backed sofas richly upholstered in damask-stamped chenille velvet have been included to soften the effect.*

OPPOSITE: *Interior designer Michael Chatterton's flat seems more Italian than English. The dramatically decorated hallway with its oversized paintings recalls the splendour of a Roman palazzo.*

LEFT: *The drawing room, like the hall, is papered with ochre-coloured wallpaper to give the effect of Italianate marble.*

ABOVE: *A marble lamp base contrasts with the faux marble walls.*

LEFT: *Carefully chosen artefacts, a bust, framed seals and drawings add to the classical mood.*

RIGHT: *Brushed silver metallic walls provide a perfect textured background for the eclectic mix of furniture in the drawing room of Peter and Felicity Osborne's present house in London. Contemporary classics such as a metal and bronze table by Mark Brazier Jones and a leather coffee table are offset by period pieces.*

ABOVE: *Period and modern mix happily in the Osbornes' sunshine-yellow hallway. A wrought-iron mirror by Mark Brazier Jones sits on an eighteenth-century French stone fireplace.*

RIGHT: *Decorator Jenny Armit has given great thought to the curtains throughout the house. Here a deep, horizontally pleated heading is used on the silk drawing room curtains which are hung from a silver-leafed pole.*

LEFT: *Colours and fabrics have been carefully chosen to heighten the impact of the entrance hall. An antique Russian settle is upholstered in a checked moiré weave, while vibrant orange silk damask curtains are lined with a contrasting yellow plain silk.*

ABOVE: *The hallway of Antony Little's former country house is symmetrically hung with lithographs by the nineteenth-century naturalist Audubon.*

OPPOSITE: *Antony often uses striped wallpapers in hallways to provide an interesting and yet neutral background for pictures and prints.*

CREATING THE MOOD

At the heart of classic style is a mood of luxury and elegance, a love of the well crafted, the comfortable, even the opulent. Every detail of a classic interior is carefully planned, its effect designed to contribute to the finished look. From the furniture down to the last tassel, nothing is left to chance.

By its very nature, such a designer-decorated room is the antithesis of an organic look that has evolved over a period of time – these rooms are often decorated from floor to ceiling. The effect may sometimes appear effortless, but the attention to detail is painstaking. Meticulously swagged and trimmed curtains, comfortable upholstery, specialized paint finishes and interestingly grouped pictures all play their part.

STRIKING PATTERNS AND COLOURS

The proportions, architectural features and period of a room, as well as the nature of the furniture used in it, determine the amount and scale of pattern that can be used successfully in wallpaper and textiles. The higher the ceilings, the bolder the pattern can afford to be. If you are not sure of the correct scale for pattern and furniture, it's a good idea to err on the generous side, as this will make a room more memorable.

If a room lacks architectural detail, try saturating it with bold pattern – the effect can be as striking as elaborate cornicing or intricate mouldings. In seventeenth and eighteenth century European interiors, one pattern printed onto damask or chintz was often used all over a room; nowadays, a similarly striking effect can be achieved with Regency striped wallpaper and subtly striped upholstery. Continuing the pattern over the ceiling will make a room seem more intimate and can create an almost tented effect, as in the hallway of the French country house shown on the right and opposite, which has been completely decorated with a soft purple and green striped paper.

Like patterns, the choice of colours is ultimately personal but is affected by the period and style of the room, and also its aspect – whether it is dark or light, and north- or south-facing. Yellow is a good choice for sunny, south-facing rooms. It calls out to be used in a positive way, and when it is, the result is remarkable. True yellows glow in sunshine. The bright yellow neoclassical sitting room created by the Regency architect Sir John Soane for his home, and the saturated yellow of Nancy Lancaster's London drawing room, are unforgettable. The palest shades of yellow can look insipid, however, so are generally best avoided; you will get a better effect by teaming a strong yellow with cream or white.

Warm, rich colours will add depth and intimacy to colder, north-facing rooms, successfully compensating for the lack of warm sunlight. Red, the richest colour of all, is often associated with luxury and opulence – red damask, for example, was traditionally stretched over the walls of grand state rooms. It is a demanding colour to work with but is striking when used well. A small room can take on a jewel-like intensity with red-painted or papered walls. But it is as an accent colour that red is more frequently used and really comes into its own. A sofa covered in figured red damask immediately looks significant. Clear red or crimson cushions in rich silk taffeta will add an extravagant air to a classic, cream-coloured drawing room, while a red linen lampshade or rich red Turkish carpet can have a similar effect.

Green too will add warmth to a room short on natural light. In nature, green often acts as a foil for other plants – think of vibrant red or pink peonies against soft green leaves, or the purple flower heads of rosemary on spiky silver green stems. In the same way, it is one of the most versatile colours in decorating. The duller shades of green, such as olive and sage, work well in traditional interiors, perhaps offset by soft lavender, lilac and purple. These muted shades are peaceful and relaxing, making them an ideal background colour for a library or study, particularly when combined with richly textured fabrics such as damask and figured velvets. Deep lemon yellow is a good foil to stronger tones of vibrant green (a combination that looks particularly effective when used as a check) while touches of gold will make a scheme that is based on the green spectrum positively sparkle.

ABOVE: *A bold use of colour and contrasting pattern makes a striking view through a series of rooms from the entrance hall to the garden.*

OPPOSITE: *A soft purple and green striped wallpaper is carried up to the ceiling in the entrance hall of this French country house.*

RIGHT: *A delicate late eighteenth-century English chinoiserie dressing table is framed by full-length curtains.*

OPPOSITE: *Felicity Osborne deliberately chose coral pink as a feminine yet strong and assertive colour for her country bedroom. An adaptation of a rustic French eighteenth-century linen print, it contrasts well with checked silk and Edwardian lace.*

BELOW: *Parchment wool damask curtains and fabric-covered walls edged with a contrasting green cotton trim provide a clean, fresh background to this classic bedroom. The lively print on the half-tester is lined with pale cream silk.*

CRUCIAL DETAILS

A feeling of luxury, so closely associated with the classic interior, depends upon a meticulous attention to detail. As much thought is given to lighting and personal touches – pictures, prints, flowers – as to the framework of furniture, fabrics, wallpaper and paint.

Lighting is essential for creating atmosphere and yet it is one of the most difficult things to get right. Classic interiors demand subtle lighting and period fittings, and table lamps are generally the most successful solution. Decorative as well as functional, they provide accents of light which will emphasize the quality of fabrics and highlight features within a room. The shades are as important as the bases. Pleated silk shades, grander and more formal than card shades, will diffuse the light and soften the overall effect. Patterned cotton or chintz trimmed with a fan edge can look charmingly feminine used as a shade, while the more austere lines of a plain linen shade can be softened with a fringe.

Collections of pictures or photographs will instantly personalize a room, however grand it may be. In the eighteenth century, when print rooms were the height of fashion, groups of prints would be linked by trompe l'oeil paper ribbons and garlands of flowers and leaves. This highly decorative treatment can be modified today by hanging pictures with taffeta ribbons, tied into bows or rosettes. Or try introducing a decorative piece of wood or gesso carving to a wall of pictures, to add a third dimension. The most successful 'wallscapes' mix different shapes and sizes of picture. Hang more dominant pictures towards the top and smaller images at eye level. Unusual collections, such as antique seals, can be framed to great effect. Simultaneously classical and masculine, they are ideally suited to a library or study.

Fit the painting to the location. Entrance halls and staircases can take striking images, boldly framed to catch the eye as people pass by. Still lifes of fruit, vegetables and botanical engravings seem well suited to a dining room – the stronger the image, the more effective it will look by candlelight. The nature of the painting or print will also affect the overall atmosphere of the room. The detailed botanical studies of the eighteenth and nineteenth centuries, for example, will blend perfectly with a period interior, while architectural prints, symmetrically hung, will lend an air of classical restraint.

EXTRAVAGANT CURTAINS

Curtains are so often the focal point of a room, the element that creates the strongest visual impression. Dressing a window or a bed can be one of the most exciting challenges for a decorator. Not surprisingly, it was the French who, in keeping with the flamboyance of the Empire style, were responsible for establishing the haute couture of curtain treatments in the late eighteenth and early nineteenth centuries. Sketchbooks of designs, inspired by the work of the Parisian upholsterer d'Hallevant, chronicled the most lavishly draped, fringed and swagged confections imaginable. These indulgent neoclassical concoctions of raw silks, muslins and fine cottons are still an inspiration today, although the translations are on a more modest scale.

RIGHT: *Christopher Nevile has decorated this bedroom in a formal French fashion. The* bâteau-lit *is draped with rich ikat silk curtains lined with a toning plain silk.*

ABOVE: *Lavish curtains and ruched blinds (shades) combine ikat and striped shot silk with printed cut velvet and deep fringing.*

Elaborate treatments involving formal swags and tails are best-suited to large, high-ceilinged rooms with tall windows. Yet they can still create an impact in a smaller room, so long as a sense of balance is achieved – the finished curtains must be in proportion to the scale of the architecture and decoration. The grander the architecture, the more ornate the curtains can afford to be. Getting it right is simply a question of balance.

The very nature of swags and tails means that they can look quite formal. For a softer effect, allow the curtains to drape onto the floor or leave fabrics such as silks unlined. Treatments in which the curtains are caught back much higher than normal can look particularly decorative.

LEFT: *Tessa Kennedy wanted the spectacular dining room of her country house to look like a Victorian bazaar filled with treasures from Oriental travels, so she hand-painted the ceiling and used richly coloured silks for curtains and cloths.*

RIGHT: *Folded silk napkins add an exotic finishing touch to the individual place settings.*

LEFT: *The restrained elegance of Christopher Vane Percy's Georgian drawing room seems more Continental than English. The eau-de-nil panelled walls have a gesso finish, achieved by painting and combing the panels and then sealing them with beeswax.*

ABOVE: *Pale striped seersucker silk curtains hang from ornate Victorian cornice boxes which have been painted and gilded to match the walls and gilt cornice (crown molding). Decorative fringes and tassels add an eighteenth-century feel.*

RIGHT: *With scrupulous attention to detail, even the ornate tasselled tiebacks fit the period feel of the room.*

TRADITIONAL WITH A TWIST

The immense choice of fabrics available today makes it possible to improvise and give traditional window treatments an exciting new dimension. A classic style with an unconventional fabric, for example, will look fresh and smart. Experiment with sheer white cotton, swagged and caught with rosettes. Mix different textured fabrics: silk taffeta swagged over a curtain pole, with linen or printed cotton curtains, becomes a contemporary classic. Nancy Lancaster, the doyenne of country house decorating half a century ago, would appliqué borders of antique textiles onto new curtains and cushions, a striking effect much imitated by professional decorators today, as in the example on page 49.

Classic curtains demand sophisticated headings. A goblet heading defined by fabric-covered buttons or a smart pinch-pleated heading is elegantly restrained and is often all that is required when using richly patterned silks and damasks. A more elaborate hand-smocked heading is a softer alternative for a bedroom. Bedroom curtains can also look charming with simple gathered or pencil-pleated headings, particularly if interest is added to the curtain with contrasting binding, braid edging or a plain or patterned border.

ABOVE LEFT: *A glorious Zeigler carpet was the starting point for this interior, its muted tones linking the many different patterned fabrics.*

ABOVE: *A late nineteenth-century Egyptian revival table becomes a focal point when dramatically framed by blue shot silk damask curtains.*

OPPOSITE: *The Osbornes' love of the decorative arts is clearly visible in the drawing room of their former London house. Here a Fornasetti screen is offset by an eighteenth-century Indo–Portugese table.*

RIGHT: *A charcoal distressed striped wallpaper provides a subtle background for an elegant early nineteenth-century Biedermeier desk and Art Nouveau chair. An eighteenth-century steel club fender is covered with a woven check.*

Curtain tracks can be concealed by painted, papered or fabric-covered pelmets (cornices). Poles of polished or painted wood or metal with carved or gilded finials, often used in interiors of the seventeenth and late nineteenth centuries, will suit strong room schemes.

The quality of any window treatment rests on its attention to detail. The lining of a curtain, which usually receives very little thought, can be used to emphasize the quality of the main fabric. Linings of swags and tails are often in a different colour, but a contrasting texture of fabric can be used as well. A sheer voile seems even more diaphanous when juxtaposed with a chenille or epinglé velvet. An unexpected combination of patterns can be equally effective; a neutral check looks wonderful when used to line a natural-coloured silk.

You only have to examine an interior decorated by a professional to understand the importance of trimmings. Never before has there been such an array of fringes, braids, ropes and tassels to choose from. The difficulty lies not in deciding what to use but in knowing when to stop. Swags and tails (cascades), pelmets (cornices) and curtains can be trimmed with a deep bullion fringe or emphasized by a more delicate fan edging, while knotted rope will add texture and interest to a heading. Translucent voile undercurtains with a frivolous tasselled edging can be held back with rope tiebacks finished with large, extravagant tassels.

Equally lavish effects can be created out of fabric. Rosettes, either in the same fabric as the curtain or echoing the lining, make a decorative addition to a formal heading. Scalloped and pinked edges, ruffles and ruching, which owe as much to period eighteenth-century costume as they do to decorating, create an equally sumptuous look.

RICHLY TEXTURED FABRICS

The sense of luxury created by a classic room necessitates richly textured fabrics such as silks, velvets and damasks which evoke a feeling of splendour. The texture of the materials is all-important, for a skilful combination of fabrics will bring a room to life. The success of a decorative scheme is dependent upon this very combination of different textures, the cool quality of reflective surfaces such as chintz and silk balanced by the warm tones of light-absorbing weaves. That is why a classic combination of silk, taffeta or chintz curtains with furniture upholstered in damask, velvet and chenille, interwoven with antique textiles, cannot fail to please. It is a mixture of fabrics that avoids any attempt at coordination, but is subtly linked by a shared colour palette.

RIGHT: *The private dining room of London's Cobden Club, decorated by Matthew Godley, is a symphony of pattern and texture. The textured wallpaper provides a soft, almost three-dimensional background for rich silk ikats and cotton weaves.*

DISTINCTIVE FURNITURE

Traditionally upholstered furniture can successfully be covered in a variety of fabrics. A classic wing chair, for example, which looks completely traditional when covered in a figured damask, becomes quite contemporary when upholstered with a sharp stripe. The patterns and textures of the fabrics within a room can vary, so long as the designs are linked to a colour theme, which will make them work as a cohesive group. Decorators often use a stripe or check to connect different patterns effectively. Another common practice is to link furniture visually using matching piping and braids.

Piping is, in fact, one of the easiest ways to elevate a design from the ordinary to the memorable. The shape of the piece of furniture will be clearly defined by contrast piping. This is normally achieved with cotton or silk cord, although the same cotton or linen as the main fabric may be used provided it is two shades lighter or darker to create a contrast. Self-piping will automatically create a more informal, understated look.

LEFT: *A classic stencilled damask design of distressed gold on a rich ruby ground is a perfect foil to the deep wood panelling of this Normandy château.*

BELOW: *Felicity Osborne based the design of this traditional Gunton chair on an eighteenth-century wing chair. Covered in striped cut velvet, it becomes a modern classic.*

Other trimmings also determine the overall look. A bullion fringe, for instance, much used in Early Victorian days, makes as strong a masculine statement as nailing does on leather or antique needlework.

Some of the most effective classic schemes mix modern upholstered furniture with antique pieces. However faithful one would like to be to a period look, too correct a reproduction can make a room cold and uninviting. A Georgian sofa might look wonderful but comfort is not one of its strong points – upholstery, as we now know it, was not developed until the mid nineteenth century. At any rate, the juxtaposition of old and new, comfortable sofas and armchairs with antique pieces, adds individuality and interest to a scheme. Adding a Queen Anne wing chair or a Regency chaise to a room will have the same effect as a fine painting, providing a focal point and a sense of tradition.

The solid lines of English furniture are often complemented by the more delicate profiles of French antiques. A traditional sofa flanked by Louis XVI chairs, for example, is a popular combination. Such period wooden-framed chairs are often upholstered in two different fabrics – perhaps a patterned weave or print with a coloured stripe, check or plain fabric.

LEFT: *Interior decorator Melissa Wyndham chose to underline the simple grandeur of the library at Mottisfont Abbey in Hampshire with a few well-chosen pieces of furniture.*

ABOVE: *The elegant shape of a Regency sofa is emphasized by a sophisticated velvet.*

OPPOSITE: *The richness of green damask chenille contrasts with antique tapestries and needlepoint in this dining room decorated by Christophe Gollut.*

BELOW: *An antique tapestry panel, appliquéd as a border onto the damask chenille, is a device often used by professional decorators to provide a contrast of colour and texture.*

ABOVE: *The infinitely adaptable star wallpaper takes on a classic look when combined with traditional furniture and swagged curtains.*

RIGHT: *There is nothing understated about the atmosphere of this dining room. The gold heraldic design of the wallpaper is a perfect foil for extravagant Venetian glass and armorial china.*

BELOW: *A collection of antique armorial china means that every place setting is quite individual.*

CLASSICAL WALL TREATMENTS

For the traditional decorator the seventeenth and eighteenth centuries are a rich source of inspiration for wall treatments. Surface textures were often not what they seemed, and architectural features were tricked out of flat surfaces. Faux panelling, with its realistic-looking painted shadows and highlights, was combined with convincing imitations of marble and stone, while doors were grained to look like mahogany, marbled or even lacquered. In a flourish of decoration for decoration's sake, trompe l'oeil carved frescoes, garlands of flowers and borders of braid all blurred the division between reality and illusion.

These painted effects are an integral part of a classic approach to decorating. They can be recreated with modern materials, paints and glazes or achieved with wallpapers that effectively imitate the finishes perfected three hundred years ago. Wallpaper borders can take the place of classical mouldings or imitate a painted frieze of flowers or a rococo swag of ribbons.

Many of the earliest wallpapers copied the very fabrics they were destined to replace. Damasks, silks, brocades and printed cottons had all been used to cover walls in the seventeenth century before the advent of wallpaper. Today the subtly patterned papers that give the impression of fabric or of a specialist paint finish provide an ideal starting point for a classically decorated room. They add texture without being overpowering and are a perfect background for paintings and prints.

Other designs based on archive prints capture the quality of early hand-blocked wallpapers. There are patterns inspired by the eighteenth-century vogue for chinoiserie, the decorative vignettes of classic toile de Jouy patterns and large-scale floral and gothic motifs. Any will add interest to featureless walls and make a dramatic statement in the right setting.

A richly textured background can also be created with fabric. Plain or textured material can be battened to the walls and edged with a decorative braid or rope or hung loosely in gentle folds to create an almost tented effect. The choice of fabric determines the finished effect. A figured damask will envelop a room, creating a rich, intimate atmosphere, while a patterned chintz will appear lighter and fresher. A rope border, in a coordinating or contrasting colour, can be used to edge fabric-covered walls or to highlight the contours of interesting details, such as an unusual fireplace.

RIGHT: *The classic combination of forest-green figured damask chenille and shot silk has been used to great effect in this London dining room cum library, decorated by Lady Victoria Waymouth.*

ABOVE AND RIGHT: *East meets West in this richly exotic library, part of the room shown on the previous page, decorated by Lady Victoria Waymouth. Portraits of Eastern potentates hang in a quintessentially English setting. Silk ikats and cut velvets are used to cover bolsters and cushions and to provide a textural contrast to the damask chenille covering the walls.*

DESIGNERS' SCHEMES

Lady Victoria Waymouth's predilection for rich fabrics and textures has transformed the library of the house on pages 52–55. In a room that is as reliant on the contrast of textures as on combinations of pattern and texture, every detail has been carefully planned to contribute successfully to the mood of period opulence. The background of figured forest green damask chenille is balanced by reflective sheer silks and the softness of ribbed velvet. Deep green walls, curtains and upholstery are offset by intense red cushions and bolsters. Equally effective schemes could have been achieved with combinations of red or blue fabrics, such as those shown opposite, highlighted with gold.

ABOVE: *Some of the fabrics used in the room on pages 52–55 are shown above. For a similar effect, you could use any of the fabrics, wallpapers, borders and trimmings shown opposite. The pattern names are given in the captions, while the collections to which they belong and the reference numbers, are given on page 174.*

REDS

FABRICS: *1 Braganza Check 2 Titania
3 Braganza Damask 4 Cuenca
5 Eglantine 6 Little Hussar 7 Tamar
Weave 8 Palanquin 9 Verona*

WALLPAPERS/BORDERS: *1 Balthazar
2 Catalpa 3 Eugenie
4 Pompadour 5 Couronne
6 Gimp, Bernadotte, Melchior*

TRIMMINGS: *1 Chenille Bullion
2 Diamond Braid 3 Fan-Top Fringe
4 Small Bullion 5 Wide Braid
6 Chenille Seersucker
7 Seersucker Braid*

GREENS

FABRICS: *1 Derby Chenille
2 Newmarket 3 Catria
4 Cuenca 5 Patara 6 Ghillie
7 Sunstitch 8 Titania*

WALLPAPERS: *1 Circe 2 Merlin
3 Bernadotte Stripe 4 Turquine*

TRIMMINGS: *1 Chenille Braid
2 Chenille Rouche 3 Picot Braid
4 Fan-top Fringe*

BLUES

FABRICS: *1 Merlin 2 Little Hussar
3 Ghillie Wool 4 Rosina 5 Iona
Large Check 6 Callisto 7 Nomad
Stripe Moiré 8 Braganza Damask*

WALLPAPERS: *1 Bakhmal 2 Artemis
3 Cathay 4 Caspar*

TRIMMINGS: *1 Piping Cord 2 Bullion
3 Cable Rope 4 Narrow Braid*

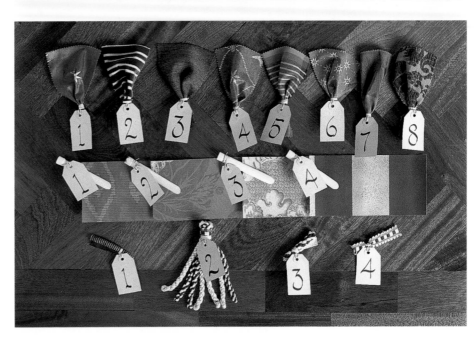

CHAPTER TWO

City

◆ ◆ ◆

ABOVE: Mother-of-pearl buttons are used as a decorative detail on vibrant silk cushions.

LEFT: Glittering jewel-like shades add accents of colour to this eclectic drawing room decorated by Kelly Hoppen. Silk, chenille, cashmere and fur are contrasted in an unconventional and thoroughly contemporary mix of textures.

PRECEDING PAGES (MAIN PICTURE): When Christopher Nevile converted an Edwardian bank into a modern apartment, he turned the whole ground floor into a grand reception room. The eclectic mix of modern furniture and contrasting colour scheme are well suited to the strong architectural character of the building.

PRECEDING PAGES (INSET): A geometric voile is lined with a stonewashed cotton in an interesting contrast of colour and texture.

CONTEMPORARY, 'CITY' STYLE need not mean stripped-down minimalism, but it is a fresh approach to decorating: a new look at the way papers and fabrics can be used to suit a modern urban lifestyle, a fresh appreciation of colour and texture, a reappraisal of furniture and furnishings. It shows a love of simple basic designs that are both functional and sophisticated.

There is a vitality and energy about the best contemporary interiors which stem from an appreciation of the qualities of light and space. The designs and colours are stronger, the decoration crisper and sharper-edged. Fabric is not used for fabric's sake, but rather for the intrinsic value of its texture and individual character. The overall effect may be simpler and less cluttered than a richly decorated room, but that does not mean it will take less thought and planning. When you simplify and pare things down, colour, pattern and texture are all given more emphasis – every detail counts, down to the final jug of flowers.

BELOW: *A modern sofa in interior decorator Mark Zeff's New York showroom is upholstered in beige silk, with the outline emphasized by a contrasting red piping.*

RIGHT: *An inset square panel of oyster silk adds shape and interest to these unlined velvet blinds.*

RIGHT: *Kelly Hoppen used changes in texture and shape rather than colour to produce an atmosphere of calm serenity in this bedroom, which is decorated entirely in neutral shades of ivory and cream.*

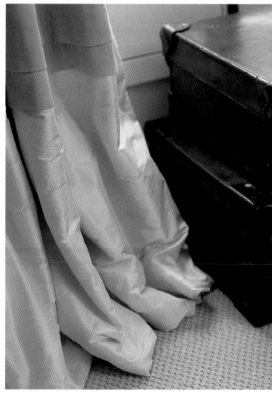

ABOVE: *A deep border of ivory silk provides a subtle contrast of colour and texture to the natural stonewashed cotton curtains.*

OPPOSITE: *Silk and suede cushions rest against a gilt mirror, which makes an unusual and striking bedhead.*

BELOW: *A deep red border adds definition to smart cream curtains by Mark Zeff.*

QUIRKY DETAILS

Make a statement with idiosyncratic touches; an unusual low-voltage modern lamp without a shade can be just as effective in an understated room as swathes of taffeta in its classical counterpart. Arrange flowers in simple containers like metal buckets, or as single stems in individual glass vases. Grow spring bulbs in pebbles or among shells. Whitewash a conventional flowerpot and plant it with a single arum lily.

Contemporary photographs are becoming increasingly popular as an interesting alternative to paintings and prints. Combine black-and-white twentieth-century pictures with quality hand-made frames, in ebonized wood or hammered silver, which suits strong graphic images perfectly.

STRONG TEXTURES AND PATTERNS

The texture of fabrics, flooring and objects is a major factor in the atmosphere of a room. Although rough textures like wood, wicker or matting are associated with the country look, they can also be used to great effect in a contemporary urban interior. There is an inherent simplicity about a room decorated with these natural textures and neutral shades. Subtle wallpaper or paint effects, used with linen and voile, are particularly suited to many contemporary interiors, while the textures of metal, glass or marble suit a streamlined modern mood.

LEFT, BELOW AND RIGHT: *Black-on-black striped wallpaper dictates an unconventional neutral colour scheme in designer John Wright's drawing room. The emphasis on texture is clearly shown by the successful mix of wood, metal and glass.*

Combinations of different textures are very important in contemporary decorating. Crisp cottons and linens will look fresher when used alongside deep woollen throws and blankets. A woollen fabric seems softer when trimmed with a border of calico or leather. Voile curtains look even more delicate when edged with a patterned cotton.

Texture takes on a particularly important role in a simple interior where furniture and objects are minimal. The injection of natural textures will bring a

ABOVE: *The introduction of moiré checked curtains softens the overall effect in the Osbornes' kitchen.*

OPPOSITE: *Stainless steel is combined with granite worktops and a stone floor for maximum textural interest.*

TOP RIGHT, CENTRE RIGHT AND BOTTOM RIGHT: *Sliding doors framed with sculpted, sandblasted wood and lined with padded moiré checked fabric create an unusual and decorative partition between the dining room and the kitchen.*

room to life and will make it more comfortable and inviting. Whether it is the rough texture of a woven basket or a piece of sandblasted wood, or even something as simple and tactile as an earthenware bowl on a white cotton tablecloth, it will underline the simplicity of the overall effect.

Strong pattern must be used with conviction too. Mix patterns rather than matching them. Combine different geometric motifs; checks and stripes, for example, will sharpen each other. The scale of patterns is important, too: offset large checks with smaller plaids in the same colour range.

The simplest decorative devices are often the most effective. Line a large checked or plaid throw with a smaller check or plaid, or simply reverse the colours of a two-tone check. Another idea is to back a paisley chenille with a striped cotton for a contrast of pattern and texture.

ABOVE: *The muted tones and chenille texture of this printed cotton make it a perfect choice for a contemporary sofa.*

OPPOSITE: *This Osborne & Little sofa is upholstered in a chunky ribbed velvet corduroy. Moiré checked cushions link the sofa to the curtains.*

ABOVE RIGHT: *Stylized silhouettes of African flora and fauna provide unexpected but very decorative bands of pattern on this voile.*

LEFT: *A bold contemporary paisley-printed chenille covers the walls of the Osbornes' bedroom. Creamy-yellow silk, padded wattle cushions provide a contrast to the chunky texture of a ribbed velvet sofa.*

RIGHT: *The shaped headboard is upholstered in a small patterned weave that was inspired by the design of Argyll socks.*

BELOW: *Sumptuous creamy-yellow silk-lined curtains with a wattle heading lighten the effect of the chenille-covered walls.*

ABOVE: *This practical laundry basket, which is made from chenille, was designed to match the walls of the adjoining bedroom.*

ABOVE RIGHT: *Voiles are becoming increasingly popular and can be prettily patterned as well as plain.*

LEFT: *Spearmint-coloured walls set the tone for the Osbornes' light, fresh bathroom. Natural materials abound; the bath is set into opaque glass and the floor is natural stone.*

RIGHT: *A patterned voile curtain is a good solution for a bedroom window, being both decorative and practical.*

BALANCE AND SUBTLETY

On walls, use simple motifs that relate to those of the soft furnishings – balance a star-patterned wallpaper, for example, with an equally straightforward check fabric. Strong-coloured geometrics combined with simple floral prints work well in bedrooms and kitchens. Checked cushions or slipcovers tied onto dining chairs will add freshness to an urban dining room.

Introduce subtle pattern and texture with self-patterned weaves. Available in many toning shades, they are now even more popular than printed upholstery fabrics, as they introduce texture without the conflict of a dominating pattern.

CONTEMPORARY COLOUR

Be prepared to make bold use of colour, for it is the easiest and often the least expensive way to transform a room. Colour can add interest to a featureless interior or it can be used to enhance rich architectural details. It can also make a space seem larger or smaller. The cool, distancing shades of blue, green and grey add dimension to a room, while warm, bright reds, yellows and terracottas create a more intimate effect. The relationship between the colour of the walls and the ceiling can also alter the proportions of a room visually – the lighter the ceiling, the higher it will appear, whereas a dark ceiling and light walls will decrease the apparent height of the room.

ABOVE: *A modern tufted Laurier rug patterned with a line of large-scale leaves adds interest to a landing.*

RIGHT: *These skilfully designed bookcases have been built to follow the curve of the wall. The strong shades of yellow, mauve and aqua are reflected in the needlepoint Nantucket rug.*

INTERACTION OF COLOURS

The colours of paints, papers and fabrics can be matched or contrasted to create different atmosphere and styles. Professional decorators often introduce accents of contrasting colour to heighten the effect of a colour scheme. For example, the strong, hot shades of the red/yellow spectrum will add vitality to a pale, cool colour scheme (imagine red apples against green leaves). Similarly, the sharp contrast of cool blues and greens will make a warm scheme even more vibrant. The skill lies in knowing just how much contrasting colour to introduce. Accents of colour provided by cushions, slipcovers or throws are often enough to bring a scheme to life, although occasionally something as simple as a bowl of red apples or jug of daffodils may be all that is needed.

The way we decorate our homes is as subject to fashion trends as the way we dress. Every decade has had its favourite colours which capture the decorating mood of the moment. The acid tones of lemon and lime, exotic orange, vibrant cobalt blue and earthy terracotta have all made their mark on fabrics and wallpapers in the 1990s.

Yet whatever the dictates of fashion, contemporary decorating will always rely on a confident use of colour – whether you choose crimson or electric blue, it must be used with conviction. Various approaches are possible. Different shades of the same colour generally look harmonious together – a room scheme built around, for example, either a palette of deep forest green and emerald, with accents of lime, or a symphony of blues from cobalt to turquoise, will be restful and sympathetic.

On the other hand, contrasting colours from opposite ends of the spectrum can look dazzling together, bringing a city interior to life. Try offsetting golden yellow with lime green and accents of blue or orange. A vibrant combination of lemon yellow and pink, reserved for the most daring, can look sensational mixed with touches of sharp, light green, verdigris metal or painted wooden furniture. Introduce these contrasting shades as blocks of solid colour – say, a pink armchair against turquoise-coloured walls, or a distressed blue cupboard against a washed background of lime green and yellow. Alternatively, use key contrast colours as accents for trimmings and accessories; throws, cushions and contemporary ceramics in strong tones will all add diversity to a scheme.

RIGHT: *The sloping roof of an attic bedroom is emphasized with a star wallpaper. Star curtains in a contrasting colour are held in position by a metal rod.*

NATURAL FOILS

One of the most important things to remember about using strong, bright colours is to balance them with a generous amount of neutral and natural tones, for vibrant tones need space to 'breathe'. All the natural tones of cream, ivory and beige provide a subtle foil for strong colours. These are the colours of wood, wicker and stone, raw silk, calico, coir matting and natural linen. There is, in fact, enough variety and textural interest within this colour palette for a neutral scheme to work well on its own. But when combining them with strong, bright colours, opt for the closely related warm, earthy shades of red and terracotta, or deep cobalt blue, as the effect of both ranges of colour is heightened by contrast. White, too, in its plethora of shades is a good foil for other colours.

ABOVE LEFT: *Skilful use of space and subtle use of colour and texture are central to Christopher Nevile's approach to interior design, as in this sophisticated modern bedroom suite he has created from a former safe in the basement of a converted bank.*

ABOVE: *Accents of earthy red upholstery and a soft green fabric-lined alcove add warmth to the neutral colour scheme of the bedroom.*

Designers who spend their days working with colour often choose to live in uncluttered, neutral spaces. Decorator Christopher Nevile, for whom good contemporary design is a preoccupation, deliberately used shades of paint ranging from white to ochre for the main rooms in the modern conversion shown on this page, to emphasize the strong architectural qualities of the building itself. For the same reason, white is often the favoured choice of minimalist decorators, who value the qualities of light and proportion above all else. Yet white is an uncompromising colour, relying for effect on the visual interest of different textures and toning contrasts, the combination of matt and shiny surfaces.

A room decorated exclusively in one shade of white could seem bland and cold. If you paint the walls with white emulsion (latex), use an off-white shade

for the woodwork. In Sweden, two or three closely toning shades of white matt emulsion (latex) are traditionally used for walls, furniture and woodwork to simulate a patina of age. Specialist paint manufacturers now produce ranges of white paints which cover the complete palette from chalk white through to oatmeal, including the range of 'dirty' whites much used by professional decorators. Like all colours, white is affected by natural light. It will seem creamy in the warmth of a south-facing room, yet will take on a bluish tinge in the cooler light of a room facing north.

The effect of white on other colours cannot be overstated. Mixed with the elegant blue-greys so closely associated with the Gustavian period of eighteenth-century Sweden, for example, white serves to underline the luminous quality of these cool tones. A decor based upon these eternally appealing interiors, with simply painted walls, bleached floors or natural matting, voile curtains and painted wooden furniture upholstered with unfussy checks, is a perfect choice for a city interior. Touches of a warm colour – a terracotta flowerpot filled with lavender, the faded tones of an antique textile – will prevent this scheme from looking cold in a north- or east-facing room.

ABOVE: *A sense of space and architecture is emphasized with an imaginative use of contrasting stone, subtly coloured walls and minimal furniture.*

RIGHT: *A grand self-supporting staircase dominates Christopher Nevile's unusual conversion linking the modern basement to the more formal reception room above.*

INTRIGUING MIXES

The colour of the fabrics that you use can be as important as those of the paint or paper on the walls. Mix shades rather than matching them to avoid a look that is too coordinated. Introduce similar or contrasting colours; line curtains with a toning colour or contrasting pattern rather than slavishly imitating the background shade of the main fabric.

Try mixing fabrics of similar colours but different textures for a subtly sophisticated effect. Dark cream brushed-cotton curtains look stunning with a deep pleated border of pale cream slub silk. Introduce a square panel of bronze silk into soft beige chenille Roman blinds (shades), or edge ivory chenille curtains with a border of brown silk. Mix suede and silk cushions or throw a cashmere blanket with a satin trim over the arm of a chenille-covered armchair.

Natural fabrics such as crisp cottons and linens, soft wools, smooth silks and sheer voiles have a tactile quality that will bring a contemporary interior to life.

LEFT: *New York designer Stephanie Stokes has decorated her own library entirely with Ottoman print fabrics by Lady Victoria Waymouth.*

ABOVE: *Symmetrically arranged prints echo the formal tailored mood of this richly decorated room.*

Some upholstery fabrics can be used for curtains, though you will need to check that curtain poles or fittings will be able to take the extra weight. Unusual effects can also be achieved with unconventional fabric such as men's suiting: a chunky tweed can look very convincing as a window treatment.

Many contemporary interiors rely on walls painted with flat emulsion (latex), but sophisticated effects can be achieved with wallpapers that imitate unconventional paint effects. Mottled metallic papers in silver, bronze and gold add colour and texture, while shiny crackleglaze finishes look almost like old Chinese porcelain, and strongly patterned abstract patterns printed onto papers resembling cut velvet make a positive design statement. Linen-effect wallpapers are perfect for providing background texture while the bold shapes of ikats and geometrics in rich, deep colours work well with natural floorboards and wrought-iron furniture.

NEW LOOKS FOR FURNITURE

A mixture of furniture can make a positive design statement. Delight in the juxtaposition of old and new: the pure lines of a modern metal or zinc-topped table with an Art Deco chair, or a Regency sofa with a modern chair. Consider using an antique iron day bed or painted Swedish-style bench lined with cushions and bolsters as a fun alternative to conventional seating.

Sofas can be traditionally upholstered or loose-covered. Loose covers can be an inexpensive way of rejuvenating a tired piece of furniture or simply a good means of injecting fresh colour and pattern into a room. Plain-coloured cottons, ticking stripes or checks, cut to fit and caught at the sides with fabric ties, will transform battered old sofas and armchairs into stylishly informal, contemporary seating. Loose covers with box- or kick-pleated corners will create a smarter, more formal effect.

There is no end of ways to dress up occasional chairs. Loose covers for metal or wooden straight-backed dining chairs can be quite simple or highly decorative. They can be fitted like a frock with buttons or bows down the back, casually tied at the sides, box-pleated, frilled, piped or edged with a bobble fringe. The hemlines on these covers can vary, too – fashionable short skirts can end above the knee or halfway between the seat and the floor, while sophisticated dressers may prefer a flowing skirt that brushes the floor.

RIGHT: *David Bentheim wanted to introduce a touch of summer into his converted Victorian dining room, so he painted the walls pale lime and dressed up Italian metal chairs in citrus-coloured silks.*

RIGHT, BELOW, BELOW RIGHT AND
OPPOSITE: *David Bentheim describes
these slipcovers as 'Versace for chairs'.
For fun he stitched on a black bobble
fringe as 'a touch of Lacroix'.*

LEFT: *A selection of plain and subtly coloured frosted glass makes a memorably modern table setting.*

OPPOSITE: *Unlined lime silk damask blinds emphasize the architectural quality of these Victorian windows.*

UNCONVENTIONAL WINDOWS

Think laterally when dressing windows – a modern look need not be conventional. If the window is interesting in its own right or if it is not important to screen the light, why not simply frame it with a wallpaper border, or paint the frame a contrasting colour and then leave it uncurtained? Alternatively, try a purely decorative approach: tie a length of voile or simply patterned cotton above the window architrave, knotted on the corners and caught in the middle. Or experiment with imaginative headings, which can transform traditional full-length curtains. A wattle heading such as that shown on page 75 looks best on a fine fabric such as silk or silk damask.

Concentrate on textural contrasts achieved through borders and trimmings. A seemingly plain curtain can be made more interesting by a wide border of contrasting material, either along the leading edge or the hem – try chenille edged with silk, or wool with a chunky cotton. The closer the fabrics are in tone, the more sophisticated the effect. A border of the same fabric but in a contrasting colour looks most effective when used as a wide band along the bottom of a curtain. Use trimmings to emphasize different textures – contrast natural dyed cotton tiebacks with wool curtains, or jute tiebacks with stone-washed cotton.

Roman blinds (shades) are a simple but effective way to dress a window. They can look either casual or more tailored. Plain cotton or linen can be edged in a stripe or gingham check or, more whimsically, stitched with dried honesty seedpods or seashells. Jewel-coloured silk looks stunning as unlined blinds with sunlight filtering through.

DESIGNERS' SCHEMES

Strong-coloured silks set the pace in the thoroughly urban dining room decorated by designer David Bentheim (pages 88–93). Glass, metal and wood stand out against a background of matt painted walls, shapes are simple and strong, and colour is handled with conviction. Citrus shades appear as bold, solid blocks of contrasting colours. This confident approach is the key to successful modern decorating. Mix any of the plain and patterned silks shown opposite with boldly checked or subtly washed wallpapers and extravagant trimmings, in toning or contrasting shades, to bring a room right up to date.

ABOVE: *Some of the fabrics used in the room on pages 88–93 are shown above. For a similar effect, you could use any of the fabrics, wallpapers, borders and trimmings shown opposite. The pattern names are given in the captions, while the collections to which they belong and the reference numbers, are given on page 174.*

ORANGES

FABRICS: *1 Palmyra 2 Pizzicato*
3 Chapan 4 Nomad Stripe Moiré
WALLPAPERS/BORDERS: *1 Steppe*
2 Sandbourne 3 Khalili
TRIMMINGS: *1 Wide Braid 2 Narrow*
Braid 3 Narrow Braid 4 Small
Fringe 5 Wide Braid

YELLOWS

FABRICS: *1 Nomad Plain Moiré*
2 Cantata 3 Jelak
4 Maracanda 5 Palmyra
WALLPAPERS: *1 Khokanel 2 Steppe*
3 Cinnabar 4 Ferghana
TRIMMINGS: *1 Piping Cord – Black,*
Piping Cord – Yellow 2 Large Picot
Braid 3 Seersucker Braid

LIMES

FABRICS: *1 Palmyra 2 Nomad Plain*
Moiré 3 Chantilly 4 Maracanda
5 Nomad Stripe Moiré
WALLPAPERS/BORDERS: *1 Summertime*
2 Weatherbury 3 Sandbourne
4 Palestrina
TRIMMINGS: *1 Picot Braid 2 Fan Top*
Fringe 3 Large Picot Braid 4 Rope
Bullion 5 Small Fringe

CHAPTER THREE

Country ◆◆◆

THE RELAXED, UNCONTRIVED ATMOSPHERE of country style is one that many people aspire to, whether they live in town or in more rural surroundings. Indicative of a way of life that is more closely linked to traditional values than its urban counterpart, it has always had a nostalgic appeal to those leading a pressurized life in the city.

Yet true country style rises above nostalgia. It is more than a dream of a beamed cottage filled with blue-and-white china and patchwork quilts, for its strength lies in its simplicity and naturalness. Country style has a timeless appeal which will continue to outlive other decorating trends because at its best it is unself-conscious.

OPPOSITE AND ABOVE: *Lady Victoria Waymouth's drawing room is filled with her own fabric prints, combined here with plain velvet chenilles.*

PRECEDING PAGES (MAIN PICTURE AND INSET): *Fresh, unassuming fabrics and wallpapers are at the heart of country style.*

ABOVE: *Opulent curtains, with a deep fringed pelmet and tasselled tiebacks, frame the view into Lady Victoria Waymouth's sunny, south-facing conservatory, which is used as a dining room during the summer.*

RIGHT AND BELOW RIGHT: *The intricate patterns and muted colours of her latest collection of fabrics are inspired by her love of Ottoman rugs.*

FAR RIGHT: *A mixture of patterned cushions reflect the predominant colours of the tablecloths.*

EFFORTLESS STYLE

Today country house style is popular all over the world. Yet the most successful country interiors, whether they are grand manor houses or modest cottages, are those which have grown up over the years – or give the impression of having done so. Pattern and texture are mixed in a seemingly haphazard way (though the effect is, in fact, often carefully planned). Fresh checks combine with fabrics and wallpapers inspired by nature, while borders imitate the stencilled friezes that would traditionally have replaced cornices (crown moldings).

Objects are practical as well as decorative. Hats, walking sticks, baskets by the back door will all be used; throws over chairs that fit beautifully into the scheme of a room may also be needed on cold winter evenings. It is this seemingly haphazard, cluttered arrangement of well-used furniture and much loved objects that has inspired a host of imitations.

The unstructured nature of country-style decorating means that every interior is highly individual. It doesn't matter whether the end result is period or rustic, so long as the underlying principles are simplicity and naturalness.

LEFT: *Antique tapestry cushions and rough woven upholstery emphasize the smooth texture of silk plaid curtains in the Osbornes' country drawing room.*

BELOW: *A subtle stone-on-stone wallpaper has been used to add background texture to this natural green colour scheme. Antique textiles, a paisley shawl used as a tablecloth and a carpet-covered ottoman were added as the room evolved.*

NATURAL TEXTURES AND COLOURS

Textures – whether of flooring, fabrics or accessories – are particularly important in a country scheme. Natural floors, such as thick sisal or chunky coir matting, tumbled limestone, or rough terracotta tiles, are a perfect, hard-wearing choice for a country home. They provide not only texture but also a good, solid, neutral base colour that underpins rather than distracts from the overall scheme.

Natural textures make a country home feel lived in. Combine smooth, matt surfaces with rough textures for maximum impact. Rough surfaces often suggest age, and weathered woods and distressed paint can be visually pleasing as well as instantly adding a rustic appeal to a new house. Imagine a pantry with smooth slate shelves above well-worn, scrubbed York flagstones; a rough willow log basket filled with kindling, sitting on polished floorboards; or beaten copper bowls on antique veneered wood, and you will see how textural contrast can bring a room to life.

Strong colours are evocative too, but the way colour is applied is often as important as the actual shade. Unusual effects can be achieved in an interior by applying the same colour to different textures. Picture cobalt blue paint peeling off a piece of distressed wood, and then think of the same shade on a piece of Chinese porcelain.

The success of a monochromatic scheme depends on just this mixture of textural effects. For example, by using warm terracotta in various tones and textures, interior designer Christopher Nevile has brought the basement room shown on the right to life. On plastered walls, woven cotton, slub silk, copper and rattan, terracotta takes on quite different tones.

SIMPLE STRIPES AND CHECKS

The days of coordinating fabrics are thankfully numbered, and the priority in decorating now is to mix not match. Plain or patterned stripes add a geometric edge to prints and florals. Unfussy ginghams, long associated with country decorating, combine just as well with floral prints, toile de Jouy and folk patterns as they do with plain calicos and linens.

Wonderfully adaptable, gingham looks ravishingly simple as a neatly tailored Roman blind (shade) or when used for unlined curtains hung from a pole, or elegantly casual when edging a lined cream-coloured curtain. Think of lining a toile de Jouy print with a woven check, hanging a gingham cotton valance over striped curtains, decorating a room entirely with plaids and checks of different scales, or combining checks, stripes and florals for a random effect, linking them by using toning colours.

RIGHT: *Christopher Nevile's tendency to use the strongest colour on the largest area is clearly evident in this dining room, where terracotta-washed walls dictate the colour of fabric and furniture in a monochromatic scheme.*

Checks look as much at home in a tiny cottage as in a grand manor. Dining chairs upholstered in different-scaled checks, the outlines defined with braid, are entirely suitable for a formal country house dining room, while a boldly patterned checked sofa fits in perfectly to a cottage sitting room.

Simple two-toned checks such as blue, red or yellow printed onto white make crisp seat pads, cushions and loose covers for chairs and sofas. They are also an excellent choice for tablecloths and napkins in a country kitchen. Complicated checks on subtle cream grounds seem more sophisticated and are probably better suited to the tailored look of fitted upholstery.

RIGHT: *Fiona Hindlip has used different scales of checks to upholster dining chairs and add an informal note to an otherwise grand country dining room.*

BELOW: *A rust-coloured corduroy sofa and print curtains are used as a foil for aqua-painted panelling and blue trellis wallpaper in the Osbornes' country study.*

CONSERVATORIES AND GARDENS

Conservatories offer a natural link between the house and the garden and can be decorated with as much attention to detail as the rest of the house. They lead the eye from the house into the garden, so should ideally be a natural progression from one scheme to another. Skilfully chosen floral prints that echo the colours and themes of outside planting will add to the impression of a continuous vista. For many people, furnishing the garden itself is also a priority.

Part of the fun of choosing fabrics for a conservatory or a garden is that you can afford to use stronger colours and bolder patterns than you might indoors,

ABOVE: *Gardening paraphernalia fills the porch of Antony Little's country house.*

RIGHT: *A simple checked slipcover on a garden chair introduces another shade of green into this leafy conservatory, which leads off from interior designer Fiona Hindlip's dining room.*

as they are less likely to conflict with their surroundings. Vibrant yellows, blues and reds, which you might avoid inside, can come alive in bright sunlight, while bold stripes and checks look good on any type of garden furniture. Heavy-duty canvas and tickings are traditionally used to cover deck chairs but striped and paisley chenilles are an interesting alternative for director's chairs (see page 165 for an example) and for deep cushions on garden benches. Plain and patterned cottons can be made into loose covers to transform the most inexpensive plastic garden chairs into elegant seating for summer dining.

BOLD, SIMPLE HALLWAYS

Simple but strong schemes are often the most successful in entrance halls and hallways, too. People often tend to neglect entrance halls and hallways when decorating, but as these are the first areas that anyone will see, they should be treated with as much respect as the main living rooms. Make a bold statement with colour or pattern. Contrast the colour of woodwork and walls – try black skirting boards (baseboards) and architraves against deep yellow painted walls (see page 26) or use a sharply defined striped wallpaper for a more classical look.

OPPOSITE: *Full-length curtains in rich pink ikat silk add interest to a long narrow hallway in Carolyn Sheffield's converted stable block.*

RIGHT: *The curtains are trimmed with a fan edging and caught back with chenille-tasselled tiebacks.*

THE TIME-WORN LOOK

The most effective country schemes are those that have acquired a patina of age and look as if they have grown almost organically over the years. This look can be difficult to achieve from scratch, but new paint can be 'dirtied' by adding a little black to achieve a faded, aged effect. Modest country cottages would traditionally have had their walls washed with a water-based distemper. The pure colour and rustic simplicity were perfectly suited to these unpretentious interiors. Distemper is today enjoying a revival among specialist painters, but the enthusiastic amateur can achieve similar results more easily using a flat matt emulsion (latex) in one of the historic colours offered by many of the leading paint manufacturers.

ABOVE: *The washed silk design of a Nomad wallpaper appears almost painted, adding a three-dimensional quality to a flat wall.*

OPPOSITE: *Dramatically patterned curtains look more decorative when caught back higher than normal.*

ABOVE: *A classical bust of the head of the Empress Josephine sits on a Regency Gothic table. The strongly patterned curtain fabric imitates an old needlepoint design for a seat cover.*

RIGHT: *Walls covered with a raspberry linen weave bordered with ecru and raspberry cotton trim provide a warm background for the Osbornes' country dining room.*

COUNTRY PAINT EFFECTS AND WALLPAPERS

Country houses, farmhouses and cottages have traditionally used subtle paint effects such as sponging or stippling on large expanses of wall to add texture. Wallpapers that simulate these popular effects are equally suitable today.

Putting pattern onto walls has always been a great decorating device. In medieval times, people would decorate the walls of their homes with tapestries or painted textiles often showing hunting scenes, as much to cover up the rough walls beneath as to delight the eye. The Elizabethans used to stencil straight onto limewashed plaster. Stencilling is still popular today, and the simple repeat designs look charming in country style interiors.

Wallpaper is the quickest and easiest way of adding pattern to walls. As the interest in wallpapers is returning after many years of painted walls, so the choice of designs is increasing. Archive designs of the eighteenth and nineteenth centuries are still being revived today and the intricate, sweeping patterns of flowers and foliage inspired by William Morris and the Arts and Crafts movement can look perfect in a period room or combined with wooden panelling. Similarly, richly patterned papers in deep shades can be just right for a study or library in a country house.

Large-scale patterned papers look stunning when used decisively. Small-scale patterns, which may look quite definite in an average-sized room, can seem almost like a texture in a large room. This may be the effect you are after, but check how it will look from the other side of the room before deciding whether to buy a particular paper.

Cottage or attic rooms look warm and intimate when covered completely with a richly patterned floral paper or a wallpaper based on a toile de Jouy fabric. (Or use the fabric itself on the walls and ceiling.) Contrasting wallpapers above and below a chair rail will help break up an expanse of flat, featureless wall.

LEFT: *Full-blown roses printed onto a moiré background give the impression of watered silk.*

RIGHT: *Kit Kemp has achieved a French flavour with a rich use of pattern in this bedroom at the Covent Garden Hotel, London. A romantic floral fabric on a moiré ground covers the walls and even a tailor's dummy.*

OPPOSITE: *Fabric designs based on patchwork and appliqué motifs blend well with antique patchwork.*

RIGHT: *Simple, unpretentious styles and uncontrived, almost haphazard combinations are part of the appeal of country style.*

BELOW: *Fabric incorporating patchwork motifs makes a charming pelmet when quilted and finished with corded piping.*

FOLK ART MOTIFS

A decorative thread that runs strongly through country style is folk art, both in Britain and in the United States. As the approach to decorating over the last decade has become less structured and more informal, so the appeal of folk art has become greater. A perfect foil for simple country furniture, folk art designs have a simplicity and artistic innocence far removed from decorative formality. Patchwork designs, for example, which were passed down from mother to daughter and from household to household, are still a source of inspiration for furnishing fabrics today.

Patchwork designs and wallpapers are a perfect addition to a country bedroom. An even more authentic effect can be achieved with such fabrics by backing them with wadding (batting) and another layer of fabric and then quilting around the patchwork shapes. This quilted fabric is ideal for bedspreads, cushions or pelmets (cornices).

Many of the inspirations behind folk art have been adapted to country decorating today. Stencil designs are another source of inspiration. Stencilling became very popular among American craftsmen in the eighteenth and nineteenth centuries, when wallpaper was a luxury beyond most people's means. They simply adapted the stencils that were used to produce expensive wallpapers and invented their own repertory of strong, simple, flat motifs, with no attempt at subtle shading. The stencils were applied straight onto plaster

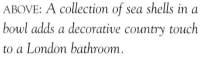

ABOVE: *A collection of sea shells in a bowl adds a decorative country touch to a London bathroom.*

ABOVE RIGHT: *A voile curtain patterned with stars lets in light while providing privacy for this romantically escapist bathroom with its painted distressed fresco and lavish marble.*

OPPOSITE: *The concept that a bathroom is a place in which to relax is carried through in Antony Little's large country bathroom with its rolltop bath and generous chaise longue. A rosette-printed border makes the spacious room seem more intimate.*

walls in colours that were traditionally as bold as the patterns. Stencilling is still highly popular today, and the simple repeat designs look charming in country-style interiors, as do wallpapers with stencil designs.

BORDERS

A wallpaper (or stencilled) border can look good with plain painted walls or with contrasting wallpaper. Simple, repetitive patterns are often the most successful. Romantic borders of leaves, flowers or swags are good choices for a bedroom, whereas abstract geometric shapes or simple primitive figures work well in kitchens, living rooms, bathrooms and nurseries.

There are no set rules about where a border should go. When used at the top of the walls it will make a room seem more intimate as the ceiling will appear lower, but it is just as effective above the skirting (baseboard) or when used in conjunction with or instead of a chair rail. Borders help to define the shape of rooms and features within them. Use one to outline a fireplace or attractive sloping ceiling, for example, or to soften austere architecture. It also provides a useful way of finishing off a room papered with a small print as it will make the wallpaper look more significant. A border can be used successfully in a nursery or child's room at waist height.

One of the liveliest developments in decorating over the past few years has been the launch of collections of paper and fabrics for children. No longer are children banished to a nursery on the upper floors – now they are making their presence felt as part of everyday life, with all that entails. Nursery tale figures march over the bed, farmyard animals stare out from borders, and memories of

summer holidays are captured in seaside and marine designs in children's bedrooms, bathrooms and playrooms. (See pages 168–171 for more ideas for furnishing these rooms.) This is the ideal opportunity to indulge all their childhood fantasies, and yours.

PLEASURES OF COLLECTING

One of the great pleasures of decorating a country house is that there is always room for collections. Whereas a modern interior may call for a few striking objects, carefully chosen for their colour, texture or shape, the very nature of an

LEFT: *The simple monochromatic scheme of this country bathroom is echoed in the drawings Antony painted as an art student.*

RIGHT: *A leaf-printed voile is tied onto an iron pole.*

BELOW: *A circular motif is carried through this bathroom from the window to the bath panel.*

LEFT: *Uzbeki silk ikats, the inspiration for the Nomad Collection, hang in the guest bedroom of Antony Little's country cottage.*

ABOVE AND RIGHT: *A newel post carved to look like an old, gnarled oak tree makes the bedroom seem like a tree-house. The swan-printed Linderhoff linen separates the bedroom from the spiral staircase.*

unstructured traditional country room imposes no such restrictions. Passionate collectors like Antony Little have free reign. Every room in his cottage is filled with things that have caught his eye over the years. Fishing artefacts, tackle, baskets and nets vie for attention with old gardening tools and miniature model furniture. These fill every available inch downstairs, while upstairs a collection of richly patterned Uzbeki silk ikats hang from oak beams.

Collections need not be grand: indeed, Antony describes his own as a 'mixture of rustic sentimental, Victorian picturesque and rural rubbish'. Simple everyday objects – spongeware bowls, rough weathered baskets, blue-and-white china – can look good when grouped together.

Nor are they expensive. Found objects, such as driftwood and pebbles from the beach, can look very effective massed on a mantelpiece. Shells can be made into a montage and framed, or used to decorate a fireplace as on page 158. The way you arrange your favourite things can add as much individual charm and character to a room as your choice of fabric and furniture.

RIGHT: *The main bedroom of Antony Little's cottage shows a characteristic profusion of pattern. A patchwork quilt is made from remnants of Osborne & Little fabrics.*

RUSTIC ACCESSORIES

Simple wooden frames suit modest, rustic rooms. These can be left natural or painted with coloured emulsion (latex) to tone or contrast with the walls. Rough wooden frames can be dragged with white paint to achieve a 'weathered' look. As an alternative to paintings and prints, try framing old sepia landscape postcards. Or combine black-and-white contemporary photographs with quality handmade frames in ebonized wood or hammered silver for a more modern graphic image. Antique lace collars or other old textiles look wonderful in rough, chunky wooden frames. Old needlework samplers are also very much at home in the cottage interior.

Fill a wall with different-sized pictures and prints. Use an unusually shaped mirror as an interesting centrepiece and arrange frames around it for an informal, relaxed look. Cottage walls can be crammed with pictures – the more you have, the more there is to look at and the more eclectic the result. Hang pictures over doorways or intersperse a series of drawings or prints with a three-dimensional carving or a group of patterned china plates.

ABOVE: *Hats, walking sticks and baskets by the front door of Antony Little's country cottage are practical as well as decorative.*

OPPOSITE (BOTTOM): *Antony is a compulsive collector, and a narrow shelf running all the way around the tiny drawing room allows him room for even more treasures.*

Make the most of the decorative qualities of plates at the table, too. The best country table settings are often the most seemingly casual. Like a delicious meal, as long as the basic ingredients are good, the recipe can be very simple. China, glass and cutlery need not be grand, but everyday pieces should be well designed and pleasing to hold and look at. A collection of unmatching antique blue-and-white china plates mixed with Victorian clear and coloured glass on a plain

ABOVE: *A simple checked cotton curtain hung from a wooden pole screens the entrance hall.*

TOP LEFT: *Antony's collection of whimsical drawings of French follies and gazebos decorates the minute hall.*

CENTRE LEFT: *A stuffed pike, one of many fishing artefacts that fill the cottage, hangs over the crowded drinks tray.*

white cloth, or simple white china and glass tumblers with crisp checked cotton table linen, are easily as effective and welcoming as a table formally set with the best damask and silver.

COUNTRY FLOWERS

Garden flowers loosely arranged in jugs or plain glass tanks will make any table seem more inviting. Raid the garden or use bunches of wild flowers – a vase of bluebells or wild cow parsley will look charmingly simple and is difficult to better. Use seasonal flowers whenever you can. Plant spring-flowering hyacinths in old blue-and-white terrines, and scented white narcissi in plain white earthenware bowls. Fill a jug with branches of early white pear blossom or branches of autumn berries. Decorate a winter table with berried ivy and delicate greenish-white hellebores. During winter, evergreen foliage like box can be cut into many interesting shapes such as spirals, pyramids and balls.

Terracotta pots can be a pretty alternative to glass or china. Try massing spikes of cut lavender in the late summer or planting pots with graceful muscari in the spring – the combination of blue and terracotta is ravishing. The deep purple nodding heads of snakeshead fritillaries make an unforgettable centrepiece; plant the bulbs in a terracotta pot and cover the soil with moss, and they will look as if they have come straight from woodland.

ABOVE: *Three different collections of Osborne & Little fabrics are mixed together in the diminutive study of Antony Little's cottage. An occasional bed is covered in patterned chenille, while the curtains are in a textured weave.*

RIGHT: *Scaled-down swags and tails, almost like decorative handkerchiefs, in a simple unlined cotton check seem perfectly in scale in the tiny drawing room.*

INDIVIDUAL PIECES OF FURNITURE

As with fabrics, it is the mix not the match of furniture that is important in country decorating, for this is what will make a room look individual. Country furniture is by its very nature simple and pleasing to the eye. The combination of strong lines and natural materials – wood mixed with metal and cane, for example – suggests an unstructured approach to decorating that is perfectly in tune with true country style.

The Shakers, whose carefully crafted furniture and tools have a beauty all of their own, proved that the functional can also be beautiful. Their ethos seems right for today when country interiors are increasingly becoming less cluttered, and a few well-chosen idiosyncratic pieces of furniture can say as much as the ornaments and trimmings of the past.

When planning a room, remember to balance the colour, size and weight of individual pieces of furniture. Never let one piece dominate completely, but add interest with a change of scale or tone. To dark furniture add something light; juxtapose a pale painted table, for example, with an old dark-leather chair. To solid furniture, add something more refined – combine a large wooden cupboard with a delicate or ornately carved chair; or traditional square dining chairs with a finely shaped gothic *étagère*.

A contrast of scale will also allow you to emphasize or diminish the proportions of a room and the various elements within it. A sense of disproportion can be as pleasing as classical symmetry. The eye will immediately be drawn to furniture that seems oversized rather than too small – a large armoire in a bedroom or a four-poster bed that fills a room will be the first thing to catch your attention, and it will be even more memorable when placed alongside a diminutive bookcase or stool.

KITCHEN FURNISHINGS

Unmatched furniture, like unmatched china, has more character than identical 'sets'. An assortment of simple chairs pulled up around the kitchen table is much more in keeping with the country lifestyle than a matching set of dining chairs.

The kitchen must always be planned to be efficient, yet it can still manage to look unfitted and relatively haphazard with the right furniture. Fitted cupboards can be combined with a dresser (hutch) or armoire, plus open shelves and a walk-in larder (pantry) if there is the space. In a traditional country kitchen, life revolves around a large farmhouse table, covered with a cloth for meals and scrubbed down to prepare food. Tiles with contemporary glazes or traditional Delft designs add colour and pattern to the walls. The combination of natural surfaces like slate, granite and marble with the colours and textures of wooden furniture and rush-seated chairs, helps to ensure that the country kitchen has all the charm of yesterday while catering for the pace of life today.

ABOVE: *A plaid wallpaper has been used to cover the ceiling of this kitchen by Brookmans Design Group. Decorators use the technique as a way of adding pattern and colour to a kitchen.*

RIGHT: *The kitchen is central to life in the Osbornes' country home. Kitchen cabinets have friezes and mouldings based on Queen Anne designs, and an eighteenth-century farmhouse table dominates the room.*

FLORAL PATTERN

More than anything, it is the profusion of pattern that makes country style stand out from other forms of decorating. The mere mention of 'country' conjures up an impression of floral prints, of roses scrambling over glazed chintz, in as great a profusion inside as they might be outside in a cottage garden.

There is nothing new about nature being an inspiration for the decorative arts, for artists have always been drawn to flowers and plants as source material. Samples of medieval crewel work are patterned with leaves and flowers, while the nineteenth-century Arts and Crafts movement, which advocated a return to the hand-crafting skills of medieval times, used native plants and birds to pattern wallpapers and fabrics. The earliest country china was crudely sponged with simple pansy-like shapes.

Today, botanical images may be more sophisticated but they are as popular as ever. Floral patterns, which can look restrained on linen and sophisticated on silk, are completely in their element when printed on fresh cotton. Chintz, the hand-printed and painted cotton that was first imported from India over three hundred years ago, has been used by decorators in both grand and modest houses to such an extent over the past four decades that it has become synonymous with English country style. This perennially popular floral fabric, normally printed on a pale ground and often glazed, is infinitely adaptable and typifies what many people find most appealing about country style. Large-scale prints are ideally suited to the elegant proportions of eighteenth and nineteenth century sash windows. The traditional cream and ivory backgrounds of these floral fabrics, which are such a good complement to the rich mahogany panelling often found in earlier houses, also work well with the limed woods found in later houses.

OPPOSITE: *Soft green and yellow floral-printed fabric adds freshness to these period windows.*

BELOW: *The pale cream background of the floral curtains serves as a good foil for rich, dark door mouldings and panelling.*

BELOW RIGHT: *A modern striped fabric stands out sharply against rich period panelling.*

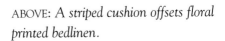

ABOVE: *A striped cushion offsets floral printed bedlinen.*

ABOVE RIGHT: *Panels of floral fabric are attached at the corners with raffia to a rustic silver birch screen.*

OPPOSITE: *The soft contours of a tailed Austrian blind are enhanced by a contrasting striped border.*

Cottage or attic windows lend themselves well to smaller-scale floral patterns. The architecture of the window can be emphasized by the soft folds of an Austrian blind (shade) or a pretty rural view framed by a shaped pelmet (cornice). A quilted pelmet can look particularly effective when the floral pattern used is printed onto checks or squares.

Some of the prettiest cottage rooms mix floral prints with lots of plain cottons and weaves, yet a room can just as effectively be saturated with pattern, as Antony Little's own cottage so clearly shows (see pages 126–133). Geometric stripes, checks and plaids are a useful foil to such an abundance of pattern, and something as simple as a striped cushion can prevent a floral scheme from becoming too cloying.

In the past, English chintzes were generally in soft colours, but the last few years has seen the emergence of more vivid blues, pinks, clear yellows and acid greens. These sharper tones can look wonderful in a modern interpretation of a country house when used with painted furniture, distressed wood and natural floors. Against such a textural background, a cushion or a simple slipcover patterned with flowers may be all that is needed and can be just as effective as yards of chintz.

A renewal of interest in the formal garden has also led to wallpapers and fabrics printed with topiary shapes and architectural garden details. Fun to use, these designs are perfect for a conservatory, where they successfully link the house to the garden. They also work well in children's bedrooms, teamed with bold checks, or in a country dining room.

INFORMAL WINDOW TREATMENTS

The current trend towards simpler unlined curtains, with looped headings or tied with tapes to a curtain pole, or a length of fabric seemingly casually draped over a rod when not drawn, captures the mood of the moment and suits the essence of country style. If a window is interesting architecturally or frames an important view, there is no need to swathe it in yards of fabric. Instead, opt for a treatment with a fixed heading: muslin swagged over the top of the window can look effective, as can a banner of brightly coloured silk caught to one side.

Curtain poles in wood or wrought iron can be cut to any size, and wooden poles left natural or painted to contrast or blend with the colour of the walls. The choice of finials is enormous and an unusual shape can add interest to an unexciting window. The type of heading will determine the formality of the finished effect, so choose simple headings for country-style interiors. Curtains can be slotted or pleated onto a track, tied to a pole with ribbons or contrasting fabric ties, or hung from rings on a plain pole. The simplest cottage window might require no more than a drop of fabric gathered onto stretchy wire.

Blinds (shades) suit almost any shape of window. Pleated or roller blinds can be used with curtains for insulation and privacy or to protect against strong sunlight. Roman blinds are particularly versatile. Plain cottons or classic stripes and checks can be neatly tailored as an attractive treatment for tall, elegant windows or drawn up in soft folds for a more rustic look.

Pelmets (cornices) and valances, if kept simple, can look charming and decorative. Try an unlined valance with a zigzag edge over silk curtains, or a quilted pelmet in a patterned fabric over plain cotton.

ABOVE: *A geometric cotton stripe in contrasting colours looks effective as a softly pleated Roman blind.*

RIGHT: *Fabric-covered buttons at the top of each pleat add decorative detail.*

FABRIC COMBINATIONS

For country interiors, choose natural materials – cottons, linens and wools – which feel as good as they look. Texture is as important as colour and pattern and is as effective in creating mood and style. Mix different textures: fine linen buttoned onto hessian makes striking hangings for a bed. Plain chintz or a gingham check can be used behind chicken wire to line cupboards in a bedroom or dressing room in place of conventional door panels.

Neutral colours, such as pale creams and whites, look elegant on a terrace or in a garden setting when offset by the deep green foliage. Natural-coloured cottons, linen unions and voiles look particularly effective used in conjunction with bleached wood or painted cane in this setting.

As the mixing of patterns, colours and textures becomes more sophisticated, delicate fabrics like voiles and muslins come into their own. Like a neutral shade in a colour palette, they can act as an important link between different materials in a busy scheme, providing the essential contrast vital to a successful interior.

ABOVE: *Natural white cotton is a good foil for green painted wicker furniture on the sunny balcony of a ski chalet in Gstaad decorated by Susie Kearley.*

RIGHT: *A topiary-patterned voile is used as a diaphanous undercurtain for unlined moiré plaid curtains.*

WARM COLOURS

Whatever your colour preferences, it is important to consider location when planning a decorating scheme. Northern climates demand warmer colours, while the bright, sharp Mediterranean shades which look so stunning when bathed in strong sunshine can look sadly depressing in a dull, wintry light.

The deeper natural shades of the earth colours – terracotta, pigment shades of ochre, burnt sienna and rich umber – are useful for adding warmth and tonal depth to a scheme. When these colours are roughly applied in bold washes or sponged to give the effect of peeling plaster, the finished effect can be quite

ABOVE: *The carved wooden furniture and antlers in this ski chalet in Gstaad are unmistakably alpine.*

LEFT: *A woven fabric reminiscent of an early American sampler is combined with a small diamond-patterned weave.*

ABOVE: A combination of patterned cotton, graphic checks and sheer voile makes an effective window treatment in this bedroom designed by Susie Kearley. A contrasting periwinkle design on plain cotton is used to cover the headboard, matching valance and pillow cover.

RIGHT: A graphic striped moiré is a good choice for a straightforward rectangular headboard.

rustic. Enhanced by the mellow tones of nature or old polished wood, the colours are well suited to a traditional country look. Yet when terracotta is teamed with acid greens and cool blues, the scheme is brought right up to date and becomes a perfect foil for contemporary country furniture in bleached woods or distressed metals.

Shades of terracotta are particularly easy to live with. They make sympathetic, flattering backgrounds and are a perfect complement, as in nature, to brighter colours. Think how simple and pleasing blue hyacinths look when planted in a plain terracotta flower pot, wrapped with raffia or tied with string.

The natural shades of cream and ivory have long been popular as background colours for the printed fabrics and wallpapers so suited to country decorating, as

ABOVE AND LEFT: *A simple floral handkerchief curtain lined with a contrasting check frames an attic window. Catching it over a covered finial at both corners is an effective and easily achievable treatment for a small window.*

they are more subtle and forgiving than a plain white ground. Decorators have even soaked fabric in tea to achieve the effect of a gently faded background. Today, however, many patterned fabrics are printed on a choice of cream or white cloth.

Natural tones of cream and ivory produce a very subtle effect. A room decorated with shades of warm yellows will instantly seem inviting, however cold the natural daylight may be. Architectural details can be picked out using a range of closely toning neutral shades. Woodwork, such as skirtings (baseboards), door and window frames, chair rails, architraves and mouldings, is traditionally painted or dragged a shade lighter than the toning walls and ceiling to give it more definition.

ABOVE AND RIGHT: *The simplicity of this attic bedroom scheme, with its blue-and-white floral printed wallpaper, painted furniture and checked cushions, is reminiscent of a Scandinavian interior.*

DESIGNERS' SCHEMES

Screen-printed blue-and-white flowers, which seem almost hand-painted, cover the walls and window of the attic bedroom decorated by Osborne & Little (see pages 96–97 and 146–147). Blue-and-white is a classic country combination, particularly in gingham checks and ticking stripes. Like blue, red becomes more homely when teamed with white, and red-and-white checks like those in the samples opposite are used in country kitchens across Europe and North America. Mellow ochres and yellows will create an altogether softer effect, particularly when combined with touches of deeper terracotta. Accents of lime green or clear blue will bring this colour palette right up to date.

ABOVE: *Some of the fabrics used in the room on pages 96–97 and 146–147 are shown above. For a similar effect, you could use any of the fabrics, wallpapers, borders and trimmings shown opposite. The patterns are given in the captions, while the collections to which they belong and the reference numbers, are given on page 174.*

BLUES

FABRICS: *1 Steeplechase 2 Mole Park*
3 Tamar Weave 4 Rosebery
5 Bluehill 6 Lornton
7 Downstaple Cross
WALLPAPERS/BORDERS:
1 Summertime 2 Picket Fence
3 Aviary 4 Polka
5 Wingreen 6 Sandbourne
TRIMMINGS: *1 Piping Cord*
2 Chenille Braid 3 Cut Fringe

PINKS

FABRICS: *1 Tinworthy 2 St Leger*
3 Brathay 4 Downstaple Cross
5 Malacca 6 Datcha Stripe 7 Picnic
WALLPAPERS/BORDERS: *1 Farmyard*
2 Safari 3 Parnasse 4 Piggy
TRIMMINGS: *1 Rope Bullion 2 Picot*
Braid 3 Piping Cord 4 Rope Braid

NATURALS

FABRICS: *1 Schoolhouse*
2 Melisande 3 Marlbury Downs
4 Mellstock 5 Button Up
6 Nantucket 7 Tinworthy
WALLPAPERS/BORDERS: *1 Animal Tails*
2 Valentine 3 Pipori 4 Tijou
TRIMMINGS: *1 Rope Fringe*
2 Diamond Braid 3 Seersucker Braid
4 Narrow Braid 5 Rope Braid

CHAPTER FOUR

Finishing Touches ◆◆◆

THE MOST SUCCESSFUL INTERIORS, whether they are traditional or modern in spirit, in the town or in the country, are those in which great attention is paid to detail. The detail can be of the simplest kind – carefully chosen braid or buttons on a cushion, the finish of a curtain pole, the trim on a chair. All will take into account the balancing of colour and texture.

The Manhattan town house shown opposite, which was decorated by interior designer Mark Zeff, shows just how all these elements will produce an aesthetically pleasing interior. This one room, decorated in a range of toning shades from oyster to beige and ochre, with accents of purple, makes use of a range of contrasting fabrics. Silk damask and taffeta are offset by chunky weaves and seersucker, while collections of carefully chosen paintings and artefacts add the finishing touch.

On the following pages you will find a diverse selection of ideas for curtains and blinds, wall coverings, cushions, seating, fun rooms, trimmings and collections. Whether simple or elaborate, they demonstrate how small details can make all the difference to the impact and stylishness of virtually any room scheme.

OPPOSITE TOP LEFT: *The symmetrical arrangement of pictures reflects the elegantly tailored atmosphere of this designer-decorated room.*

OPPOSITE TOP RIGHT: *A loose cover with a zigzag hem fitted over a metal chair adds a contemporary note to period furniture.*

OPPOSITE BELOW LEFT: *A quilted silk panel is an unusual but effective way of adding colour, texture and pattern to a wall.*

OPPOSITE BELOW RIGHT: *A softly coloured woven cotton fabric is used as a wall covering and for the full-length curtains.*

CURTAINS AND BLINDS

ABOVE: *A simple slotted curtain heading over a wrought-iron pole strikes an appropriately informal note in a bright modern bedroom filled with pattern and colour.*

ABOVE RIGHT: *Voile is normally used to produce a light, diaphanous look, but here the reverse effect has been created by interior designer Christopher Nevile, who has used a* deep red stonewashed cotton to line geometrically patterned voile curtains. *The unlined sheer undercurtain, in a smaller-scale geometric, provides a contrast of pattern and weight.*

RIGHT: *Repeat pattern and texture have been cleverly combined in this window treatment. A cool translucent white voile adds a calm note to the profusion of warm checks and prints.*

ABOVE: *These exotic designs by Lady Victoria Waymouth lend themselves well to unconventional window treatments. The richly coloured fabrics, inspired by rug designs, have been looped and draped over a wooden curtain pole. Chunky red tassels emphasize the Eastern mood.*

Finishing Touches ◆◆◆ 153

ABOVE: *A fabric-covered boss holds a swag of floral fabric in place in a country attic window. The fresh, unsophisticated fabric prevents the treatment from looking too grand.*

ABOVE: *A stainless steel wire threaded through metal eyelets serves as an effectively simple heading for these curtains designed by Jenny Armit, who adapted the idea from sail rigging.*

ABOVE: *An elegant and unusual deep heading of horizontally pleated silk adds the finishing touch to elegant orange silk curtains hanging from a silver-leafed pole.*

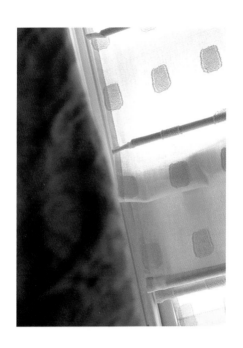

RIGHT: *A Roman blind (shade)
underlines the architectural quality of
a window. Here a voile with a
woven-in geometric pattern provides
privacy without distracting from the
shape of the window.*

BELOW AND BELOW RIGHT: *Hearts
and stars – light, translucent voiles
woven with two delicate and
romantically feminine designs.*

OPPOSITE FAR LEFT: *The clean lines of
a Roman blind made from
stonewashed cotton in three shades of
green work well with the austerity of
this Georgian interior.*

OPPOSITE LEFT: *Shot silk cannot fail to
look opulent. The very nature and
colour of navy blue silk damask shot
with yellow is emphasized by an
unlined undercurtain of yellow silk
with a woven-in star pattern.*

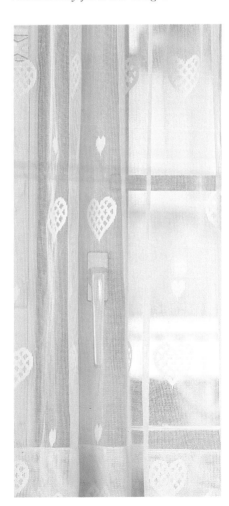

WALL COVERINGS

ABOVE: *Tartans make evocative backgrounds for other furnishings. Whether in the traditional colours of the Scottish clans or in contemporary colourways, they add richness, warmth and drama to a room. To make the most of the graphic qualities of the pattern, use it flat, as in this Norwegian hunting lodge, where a masculine blue silk plaid has been battened to the walls of an alcove.*

RIGHT: *Wallpaper borders are an effective way of defining the shape of a room. When used at the top of the wall, a border will make a high-ceilinged room seem more intimate.*

ABOVE: Bold geometric designs and lively patterns are a good choice for a kitchen. This wallpaper design of topiary trees is echoed in matching tiles behind the range.

ABOVE RIGHT: Borders can successfully frame decorative features or displays. Here, a geometric border draws the eye to two clipped topiary trees which amusingly repeat the wallpaper design.

RIGHT: A small-scale wallpaper pattern is well suited to a diminutive attic bedroom.

TOP *In a highly original treatment, snowflake-patterned wallpaper has been cut into squares and framed with a coordinating border to give the effect of contemporary panelling. Narrow strips of flat wooden moulding conceal the seams.*

ABOVE: *Here, an unusual wooden frame echoes the contemporary country scheme.*

LEFT: *Contrasting wallpapers can be used to great effect when divided by a chair rail.*

RIGHT: *The botanical theme of the decorative painted panels on the walls of this room is reflected in the choice of moss-green upholstery and flower-printed cushions.*

BELOW: *The flowing designs of a French rococo-style wallpaper create a romantic backdrop for a graceful wrought-iron bench piled high with a collection of cushions and bolsters.*

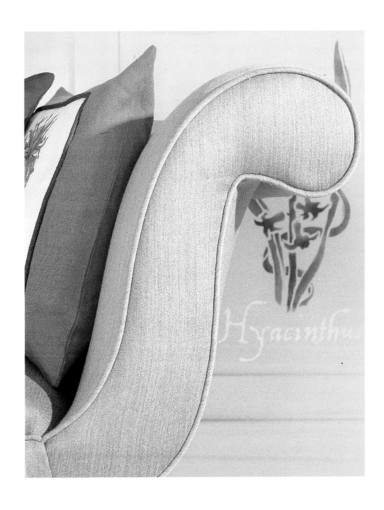

CUSHIONS

TOP RIGHT: *The graphic quality of ornamental moiré checks creates striking cushions and bolsters. As the pattern is strong, keep trimmings uncomplicated. A rope border, simple fringe or natural wooden buttons are often all that is required.*

RIGHT: *Bone discs threaded onto a leather thong make an original edging for a pair of striking cushions. Triangles of plain wool have been used to frame a square of ethnic-patterned cotton.*

BELOW: *A collection of cushions with roped and tasselled borders, gathered silk frills and chenille trimmings adds the finishing touch to a window seat. As long as the cushions share the same* colour palette, *you can mix different patterns of geometrics and plain textures with ease.*

OPPOSITE: *The look of a cushion can be changed completely by the choice of trimming or edging. If you want to achieve a dramatic effect, opt for a contrasting design – a striped border against a patterned fabric, for instance – or contrasting textures such as a silk fringe on linen. Sometimes, however, a more sophisticated effect can be achieved by using a border of similar colour and texture. A toning chenille fringe adds the perfect understated touch to the richly patterned chenille cushion, while a raised diamond-shaped ribbing adds interest to an otherwise plain silk taffeta cushion.*

TOP RIGHT: *A fine braid adds the finishing touch to a seat cover of textured ribbed velvet.*

CENTRE RIGHT: *Jenny Armit has made an assertive use of bold blocks of contrasting colour for the upholstery and cushions in this contemporary drawing room.*

BOTTOM RIGHT: *A library chair is made more decorative with an interesting envelope-shaped cushion of plain wool lined with a print and secured by a fabric-covered button.*

OPPOSITE: *Two boldly patterned cushions with brightly coloured swirls and teardrops, all in dupion silk, add a contemporary touch to a pair of traditional library chairs.*

BELOW: *The soft greens and yellows and figurative patterns of these fabrics and wallpaper are the ideal complement for the dark wood chair.*

OPPOSITE: *Rich, earthy shades of red, terracotta and green work well with dark-stained garden furniture. Rustic striped knotty cottons and moiré plaids make perfect partners for mahogany-stained director's chairs.*

LEFT: *What could be more inviting on a summer's afternoon than a hammock laden with cushions? The addition of wooden toggles, cotton rope and neat button edging gives a sharper edge to the softly distressed striped fabric.*

BELOW: *Checks and stripes look good with all sorts of garden furniture and can be used as slip covers for plastic chairs or as seat pads on more refined, wooden or metal furniture. The combination of fresh blue-and-white checks with white metal furniture is always a pleasing one.*

TABLE SETTINGS

OPPOSITE TOP LEFT: *Jewel-coloured silk ikats set the scene for a sumptuous dinner in interior designer Tessa Kennedy's country dining room.*

OPPOSITE TOP RIGHT AND OPPOSITE BELOW: *The mixture of contemporary silver by silversmith Richard Fox and modern porcelain creates an elegantly sophisticated table setting.*

RIGHT: *A dazzling gold fantasy dining room blends metallic wallpapers and gold-printed fabrics.*

BELOW RIGHT: *A theatrical dinner for two in a dining room hung with silk and filled with an abundance of pattern. The geometric design of full-length slipcovers contrasts with the large-scale floral and scenic motifs.*

FUN ROOMS

BELOW: *This child's bedroom has been decorated around a seaside/marine theme. Sea birds embellish a Roman blind (shade) and cushions, while a sturdy bucket holds shells and starfish. The candy-striped wallpaper is offset by a bold border at chair-rail height, enlivened by big spots of paint.*

BELOW RIGHT: *A more theatrical theme sets the scene in this bedroom which would capture any child's imagination. Storybook images from* Wind in the Willows *and playing-card motifs abound. Small brass bells decorate the shaped pelmet while a jester sits astride a dressing-up box.*

RIGHT: *The riot of pattern and strong colours in this bedroom would not be out of place in a New England setting. Images of folk art and Americana are captured in naive silhouettes and patchwork designs.*

BELOW: *A nursery bed is tucked into a pastel-coloured alcove, as in the interior of a Romany caravan.*

ABOVE: *Theo Osborne's bedroom is filled with vibrant colours. Cupboard doors are painted in strong greens and blues and an office chair has been given a new lease of life by covering it in cotton stripes.*

ABOVE: *Bedheads can be fun as well as practical. Here, Snap playing-card fabric gives an unexpected twist to a headboard. The fabric used for the edging is echoed in the piping on the cushion.*

ABOVE: *A contemporary tufted Chapan rug is named after the antique tribal coat the design is based on.*

RIGHT: *Glazed tiles with the design of the Snap fabric add a light-hearted touch to a child's bathroom.*

RETAILERS AND DISTRIBUTORS

FABRICS AND WALLPAPERS

UNITED KINGDOM
Osborne and Little furnishing fabrics and
wallpapers are available through leading interior
design and decorating showrooms, including:

Osborne & Little
304-308 King's Road, London SW3 5UH
Tel: 0171 352 1456
Fax: 0171 351 7813

For details of other stockists throughout the UK
and the Republic of Ireland, contact Osborne
& Little Head Office:

Osborne & Little plc
49 Temperley Road, London SW12 8QE
Tel: 0181 675 2255
Fax: 0181 673 8254

UNITED STATES AND CANADA
For information about Osborne & Little fabrics
and wallpapers, contact:

Osborne & Little Inc.
90 Commerce Road
Stamford, CT 06902
Tel: 203 359 1500
Fax: 203 353 0854

The following are the main agents for Osborne
& Little furnishing fabrics and wallpapers.
Their showrooms are open to the trade only:

ATLANTA
Ainsworth Noah & Associates Inc.
351 Peachtree Hills Avenue - Suite 518,
Atlanta, GA 30305
Tel: 404 231 8787
Fax: 404 233 5418

BOSTON
Shecter Martin
One Design Center Place - Suite 111,
Boston, MA 02210
Tel: 617 951 2526
Fax: 617 951 2418

CHICAGO
Osborne & Little
Merchandise Mart- Suite 610,
Chicago, IL 60654
Tel: 312 467 0913
Fax: 312 467 0996

DALLAS
Boyd Levinson & Company
1400-C HiLine Drive, Dallas, TX 75207
Tel: 214 698 0226
Fax: 214 698 8650

DANIA
Design West Inc. - DCOTA
1855 Griffin Road - Suite A-474, Dania,
FL 33004
Tel: 954 925 8225
Fax: 954 922 8748

DENVER
Shanahan Collection
Denver Design Center, 595 S. Broadway -
Suite 100-S, Denver, CO 80209
Tel: 303 778 7088
Fax: 303 778 7489

HOUSTON
Boyd Levinson & Company
5120 Woodway - Suite 4001, Houston,
TX 77056
Tel: 713 623 2344
Fax: 713 623 2105

LOS ANGELES
Oakmont
Pacific Design Center - Suite B647,
8687 Melrose Avenue, Los Angeles,
CA 90069
Tel: 310 659 1423
Fax: 310 659 7332

MINNEAPOLIS
Gene Smiley Showroom
International Market Square, 275 Market
Street - Suite 321, Minneapolis, MN 55405
Tel: 612 332 0402
Fax: 612 332 0433

NEW YORK
Osborne & Little Inc.
979 Third Avenue - Suite 520, New York,
NY 10022
Tel: 212 751 3333
Fax: 212 752 6027

PHOENIX
Swilley-Francoeur & Hunter
2712 North 68th Street - Suite 4000,
Scottsdale, AZ 85257
Tel: 602 990 1745
Fax: 602 990 2576

PHILADELPHIA
JW Showroom Inc.
The Marketplace - Suite 304, 2400 Market
Street, Philadelphia, PA 19103
Tel: 215 561 2270
Fax: 215 561 2273

PORTLAND
Stephen E. Earls Showrooms
208 N.W. 21st Avenue - Suite 200,
Portland, OR 97209
Tel: 503 227 0541
Fax: 503 223 1139

SAN FRANCISCO
Randolph & Hein
Galleria Design Center - Suite 101,
101 Henry Adams Street, San Francisco,
CA 94103
Tel: 415 864 3550
Fax: 415 864 5890

SEATTLE
Stephen E. Earls Showrooms
520 South Findlay Street, Seattle,
WA 98108
Tel: 206 767 7220
Fax: 206 762 5140

STAMFORD
Osborne & Little Inc.
90 Commerce Road, Stamford, CT 06902
Tel: 203 359 1500
Fax: 203 353 0854

WASHINGTON, D.C.
Osborne & Little Inc.
300 D Street S.W. - Suite 435,
Washington, DC 20024
Tel: 202 554 8800
Fax: 202 554 8808

TORONTO
Primavera
160 Pears Avenue - Suite 210,
Toronto M5R 1T2, Canada
Tel: 416 921 3334
Fax: 416 921 3227

REST OF THE WORLD
For details of worldwide distributors or agents
please contact:
The Export Office, Osborne & Little plc
49 Temperley Road, London SW12 8QE
Tel: 0181 675 2255
Fax: 0181 673 8254

ARGENTINA
Miranda Green
Cabello 3919, 1425 Buenos Aires
Tel: 01 802 0850
Fax: 01 801 6675

AUSTRALIA
Wardlaw (Pty) Ltd
230-232 Auburn Road, Hawthorn,
Victoria 3122
Tel: 03 9819 4233
Fax: 03 9819 5083

BELGIUM
Donald Thiriar Sprl
Chaussée d'Alsemberg 610, 1180 Brussels
Tel: 02 343 6400
Fax: 02 343 0633

DENMARK
Greengate Interiors
Ordrup Jagtvej 91, 2920 Charlottenlund
Tel: 39 90 40 01 / 02
Fax: 39 90 04 12

FINLAND
OY SW Lauritzon & Co AB
Elimænkatu 23, SF - 00510 Helsinki
Tel: 9 1496055
Fax: 9 1496077

FRANCE
Osborne & Little
4 rue de Petits Pères, 75002 Paris
Tel: 1 42 86 91 00
Fax: 1 42 86 90 92

GERMANY
Osborne & Little
Josephspitalstr. 6, 80331 München
Tel: 089 2366000
Fax: 089 2606001

GREECE
Ottimo
Com. Center 'Agora', 10-12 Kifisias
Avenue, Athens 15125
Tel: 01 6848107
Fax: 01 6851771

ITALY
Donati Remo & C Spa
Corso Tassoni 66, 10144 Torino
Tel: 011 437 6666
Fax: 011 437 6941

JAPAN
Manas Trading Inc.
5F Nissan Building, 4-21 Himonya,
Meguro-Ku, Tokyo 152
Tel: 03 3792 7411
Fax: 03 3792 7481

LEBANON
Linea Verde
Freeway Building, Sin El-Fil Main Road,
PO Box 16, 6174 Beirut
Tel: 1 500 469
Fax: 1 481 383

NETHERLANDS
Wilhelmine van Aerssen Agenturen
Amsterdamseweg 108-110, 1182 HH
Amstelveen
Tel: 020 640 5060
Fax: 020 640 6017

NORWAY
Poesi Interøragentur AS
Erling Skjalgssonsgt 19A, N-0267 Oslo
Tel: 22 12 81 80
Fax: 22 55 50 10

NEW ZEALAND
Wardlaw (NZ)
Cnr Railway & Leek Streets, Newmarket,
Auckland 1
Tel: 9 520 2363
Fax: 9 520 6542

PORTUGAL
Sousa & Holstein
Rua do Patrocinio 128-A, 1350 Lisboa
Tel: 01 397 8351
Fax: 01 397 1384

SOUTH AFRICA
The Fabric Library (Pty) Ltd
Old Pretoria Road, Stand 61,
Halfway House 1685, Johannesburg
Tel: 11 805 4211
Fax: 11 315 1068

SPAIN
Casa y Jardin
Padilla 32, 28006 Madrid
Tel: 91 576 1312
Fax: 91 578 0014

SWEDEN
Cadoro Agenturer AB
Nybrogatan 77, 114 40 Stockholm
Tel: 08 660 2346
Fax: 08 667 4091

SWITZERLAND
Ipso Facto
6 rue Joseph-Girard, CH-1227 Geneva
Tel: 022 342 5077
Fax: 022 343 5716

TURKEY
Felko AS
Fahri Gizdem Sokak, No 22/1, Gayrettepe
80280, Istanbul
Tel: 212 266 9921
Fax: 212 275 4287

ACKNOWLEDGEMENTS

All the photographs in this book have been taken by Jan Baldwin, except for the following which appear by kind permission:

Brookmans Design Group 134 (top): Simon Brown 5, 8, 45, 46-47, 162 (top right): © The Condé Nast PL/ Brides and Setting Up Home/ Jan Baldwin 159 (below); The Condé Nast Publications Ltd/ House & Garden/ David Montgomery 108 (top)/ Fritz von der Schulenburg 20, 21 (below), 106-107, 108-109/ Simon Upton 68-69: Michael Crocket 12, 152 (top left), 153, 157 (top), 158 (below left), 160 (top), 162 (left), 164 (top), 167, 168-169: House Beautiful/Mark Zeff design (US edition) 2, 150: The Interior Archive/ Fritz von der Schulenburg 21 (above), 28-29, 32 (top), 33, 102-103, 106, 114-115, 118-119, 120, 122-123, 134-135, 157 (below), 164 (below)/ Henry Wilson 22-23: The Interiør Magazine/ Mona Gundersen (Helena Henni Interiors)156 (top): Aline de Kostine-Kundig 59 (detail), 142-143, 144-145, 152 (top and below right): David Montgomery 52-55, 110-113, 161: The National Magazine Company Ltd/ Dominic Blackmore 157 (inset): Peter Rauter 163; Robert Harding Picture Library/Homes & Gardens © IPC Magazines Ltd/ Chris Drake 97 (detail), 154 (bottom left), 158 (top and inset), 159 (top)/ James Merrell 50 (top): Fritz von der Schulenburg 124-133: Charles Settrington 6, 13: Stock Image Production/ J. Caillaut 30-31: Barbara and René Stoëltie 44-45: Elizabeth Whiting Associates/ Andreas von Einsiedel 32 (below), 40, 41: Mark Zeff (designer) 62 (left), 67.

FABRIC REFERENCES

The names and numbers of the patterns shown on the Designers' Schemes swatchboards on pages 57, 95 and 149 are shown below.
The names of the collections are in brackets.

CLASSIC (PAGE 57)

REDS

Fabrics: 1 Braganza Check (Braganza) F861/01. 2 Titania (Alchemy) F1050/02. 3 Braganza Damask (Braganza) F860/02. 4 Cuenca (Pashmina) F1483/02. 5 Eglantine (Eglantine) F870/19. 6 Little Hussar (Hussar) F1420/05. 7 Tamar Weave (Tamar Weave) F800/03. 8 Palanquin (Pasha Velvets) F1140/01. 9 Verona (Verona Chenilles) F1330/03.

Wallpapers/Borders: 1 Balthazar (Alchemy) W1063/04. 2 Catalpa (Durbar) W1010/04. 3 Eugenie (Emperor) W591/05. 4 Pompadour (Historic Collection) W1372/01. 5 Couronne (Emperor) W590/07. 6 Gimp (Historic Collection Borders) B1390/01, Bernadotte (Emperor Borders) B593/07, Melchior (Alchemy Borders) B1070/05.

Trimmings: 1 Chenille Bullion (Chenille Trimmings) T500/01. 2 Diamond Braid (Doratura Trimmings) T527/01. 3 Fan-Top Fringe (Doratura Trimmings) T523/01. 4 Small Bullion (Doratura Trimmings) T521/01. 5 Wide Braid (Fayence Trimmings) T201/01. 6 Chenille Seersucker (Chenille Trimmings) T502/01. 7 Seersucker Braid (Doratura Trimmings) T526/01.

GREENS

Fabrics: 1 Derby Chenille (Derby) F1091/07. 2 Newmarket (Tattersall Checks) F1082/05. 3 Catria (Paradiso Weaves) F810/12. 4 Cuenca (Pashmina) F1483/06. 5 Patara (Pasha Velvets) F1141/06. 6 Ghillie (Ghillie) F1240/15. 7 Sunstitch (Sunstitch) FWS 29. 8 Titania (Alchemy) F1050/07.

Wallpapers: 1 Circe (Alchemy) W1066/08. 2 Merlin (Alchemy) W1062/07. 3 Bernadotte Stripe (Emperor) W593/09. 4 Turquine (Elysium) W727/06.

Trimmings: 1 Chenille Braid (Chenille Trimmings) T503/06. 2 Chenille Rouche (Chenille Trimmings) T501/06. 3 Picot Braid (Doratura Trimmings) T525/05. 4 Fan-top Fringe (Doratura Trimmings) T523/05.

BLUES

Fabrics: 1 Merlin (Alchemy) F583/08. 2 Little Hussar (Hussar) F1420/06. 3 Ghillie Wool (Ghillie) F1241/12. 4 Rosina (Diva) F1433/01. 5 Iona Large Check (Iona) F700/07. 6 Callisto (Gemini) F470/10. 7 Nomad Stripe Moiré (Nomad Moiré) F1280/08. 8 Braganza Damask (Braganza) F860/04.

Wallpapers: 1 Bakhmal (Nomad) W1303/06. 2 Artemis (Alchemy) W1060/01. 3 Cathay (Elysium) W725/02. 4 Caspar (Alchemy) W1064/01.

Trimmings: 1 Piping Cord (Doratura Trimmings) T520/06. 2 Bullion (Cartouche Trimmings) T510/06. 3 Cable Rope (Cartouche Trimmings) T511/06. 4 Narrow Braid (Cartouche Trimmings) T513/06.

CITY (PAGE 95)

ORANGES

Fabrics: 1 Palmyra (Lashkari Silk) F1151/12. 2 Pizzicato (Cadenza) F1414/03. 3 Chapan (Nomad) F1290/02. 4 Nomad Stripe Moiré (Nomad Moiré) F1280/05.

Wallpapers/Borders: 1 Steppe (Nomad) W1305/02. 2 Sandbourne (Wessex Borders) B1522/04. 3 Khalili (Nomad) W1308/02.

Trimmings: 1 Wide Braid (Fayence Trimmings) T201/03. 2 Narrow Braid (Fayence Trimmings) T200/03. 3 Narrow Braid (Fayence Trimmings) T200/04. 4 Small Fringe (Fayence Trimmings) T204/04. 5 Wide Braid (Fayence Trimmings) T201/04.

YELLOWS

Fabrics: 1 Nomad Plain Moiré (Nomad Moiré) F1281/07. 2 Cantata (Cantata Silks) F1400/13. 3 Jelak (Nomad) F1296/04. 4 Maracanda (Maracanda Silks) F1100/09. 5 Palmyra (Lashkari Silks) F1151/10.

Wallpapers: 1 Khokanel (Nomad) W1302/04. 2 Steppe (Nomad) W1305/05. 3 Cinnabar (Nomad) W1304/04. 4 Ferghana (Nomad) W1307/05.

Trimmings: 1 Piping Cord Black (Paradiso Trimmings) T304/10, Piping Cord Yellow (Paradiso Trimmings) T304/03. 2 Large Picot Braid (Paradiso Trimmings) T305/10. 3 Seersucker Braid (Doratura Trimmings) T526/04.

LIMES:

Fabrics: 1 Palmyra (Lashkari Silk) F1151/09. 2 Nomad Plain Moiré (Nomad Moiré) F1281/10. 3 Chantilly (Cartouche Weaves) F1320/14. 4 Maracanda (Maracanda Silk) F1100/17. 5 Nomad Stripe Moiré (Nomad Moiré) F1280/06.

Wallpapers/Borders: 1 Summertime (Scrapbook) W1194/04. 2 Weatherbury (Wessex Borders) B1520/02. 3 Sandbourne (Wessex Borders) B1522/02. 4 Palestrina (Nomad) W1300/03.

Trimmings: 1 Picot Braid (Paradiso Trimmings) T302/05. 2 Fan Top Fringe (Paradiso Trimmings) T303/05. 3 Large Picot Braid (Paradiso Trimmings) T305/05. 4 Rope Bullion (Paradiso Trimmings) T300/05. 5 Small Fringe (Fayence Trimmings) T204/08.

COUNTRY (PAGE 149)

BLUES

Fabrics: 1 Steeplechase (Tattersall Checks) F1081/03. 2 Mole Park (Scrapbook) F1179/01. 3 Tamar Weave (Tamar Weave) F800/14. 4 Rosebery (Tattersall Checks) F1080/08. 5 Bluehill (Stitchweave) F1270/03. 6 Lornton (Wessex) F1493/03. 7 Downstaple Cross (Wessex) F1496/03.

Wallpapers/Borders: 1 Summertime (Scrapbook) W1194/01. 2 Picket Fence (Scrapbook Borders) B1214/01. 3 Aviary (Scrapbook) W1196/01. 4 Polka (Charades) W845/05. 5 Wingreen (Wessex Borders) B1521/05. 6 Sandbourne (Wessex Borders) B1522/03.

Trimmings: 1 Piping Cord (Paradiso Trimmings) T304/07. 2 Chenille Braid (Chenille Trimmings) T503/07. 3 Cut Fringe (Cartouche Trimmings) T512/06.

PINKS

Fabrics: 1 Tinworthy (Wessex) F1495/02. 2 St Leger (Tattersall Checks) F1083/01. 3 Brathay (Lakeland) F1044/02. 4 Downstaple Cross (Wessex) F1496/01. 5 Malacca (Voyage) F1111/01. 6 Datcha Stripe (Cartouche) F1351/02. 7 Picnic (Scrapbook) F1173/02.

Wallpapers/Borders: 1 Farmyard (Scrapbook Borders) B1213/02. 2 Safari (Scrapbook) W1192/02. 3 Parnasse (Voyage) W1120/01. 4 Piggy (Scrapbook) W1195/02.

Trimmings: 1 Rope Bullion (Paradiso Trimmings) T300/01. 2 Picot Braid (Paradiso Trimmings) T302/01. 3 Piping Cord (Paradiso Trimmings) T304/01. 4 Rope Braid (Cartouche Trimmings) T514/01.

NATURALS

Fabrics: 1 Schoolhouse (Stitchweave) F1275/02. 2 Melisande (Diva) F1430/06. 3 Marlbury Downs (Wessex) F1497/02. 4 Mellstock (Wessex) F1494/04. 5 Button Up (Scrapbook) F1174/06. 6 Nantucket (Scrapbook) F1176/03. 7 Tinworthy (Wessex) F1495/03.

Wallpapers/Borders: 1 Animal Tails (Charades Borders) B855/01. 2 Valentine (Scrapbook) W1191/04. 3 Pipori (Durbar) W1013/04. 4 Tijou (Voyage) W1124/09.

Trimmings: 1 Rope Fringe (Cartouche Trimmings) T515/03. 2 Diamond Braid (Doratura Trimmings) T527/03. 3 Seersucker Braid (Doratura Trimmings) T526/03. 4 Narrow Braid (Cartouche Trimmings) T513/03. 5 Rope Braid (Cartouche Trimmings) T514/03.

INDEX

Page numbers in *italics* refer to captions